A Stray (Volume I)

F. W. Robinson

Alpha Editions

This edition published in 2022

ISBN : 9789356901629

Design and Setting By
Alpha Editions
www.alphaedis.com
Email - info@alphaedis.com

Contents

BOOK I.

FIGURES IN OUTLINE.

CHAPTER I.

LIFE IN GREAT SUFFOLK STREET.

It was not an evening party of the first water, or given by people of first-rate position in society, or held in a quarter whither the fashionable classes most do congregate. It was a small party—ostensibly a juvenile party—held on the first floor of a stationer's shop in Great Suffolk Street, Southwark.

Not even a first-rate stationers', had the shutters been down and the fog less dense to allow us to inspect Mr. Wesden's wares; but an emporium, which did business in no end of things—cigars, tobacco-pipes, children's toys, glass beads by the skein or ounce, fancy work, cottons and tapes. These, the off-shoots from the stationery business, the news-vending, the circulating of novels in four, five, and six volumes at one penny per volume, if not detained more than three days; a stationery business which report said had not turned out badly for old Wesden, thanks to old Wesden's patience, industry and care, say we—thanks to his screwing and his close-fistedness that would not have trusted his own mother, had she lived, said the good people—for there are good people everywhere—in Great Suffolk Street. Certainly, there were but small signs of "close-fistedness" about the premises on that particular evening; the shop had been closed at an earlier hour than business men would have considered suitable. They were wasting the gas in Mr. Wesden's drawing-room; feasting and revelry held dominion there. There had been three separate knocks given at the door from three separate Ganymedes—No. 1, with oranges; No. 2, with tarts from the pastry-cook; No. 3, with beer, which last was left in a tin can of colossal proportions, supper not being ready, and beer being liable to flatness in jugs—especially the beer from the Crown.

We watch all this from the outside, in the thick fog which made things unpleasant in Great Suffolk Street. There is more life, and life that appertains to this chapter of our history, outside here than in that first floor front, where the sons and daughters of Mr. Wesden's neighbours are playing at forfeits, romping, jumping, and laughing, and thoroughly enjoying themselves. They are not thinking of the fog, the up-stairs folk shut away from the rawness of that January night; it would have troubled Mr. Wesden had his shop been open, and led him to maintain a stricter watch over the goods, and upon those customers whose faces might be strange to him; but he had forgotten the weather at that juncture, and sat in the corner of the drawing-room, smoking his pipe, and keeping his daughter—a bright-faced, golden-haired girl of twelve—within his range of vision. The fog and the cold troubled no one at Mr. Wesden's—only "outsiders" objected, and remarked upon them to friends when they met, coughing over one, and shivering through the other, as lungs and scanty clothes necessitated. The establishment of Mr. Wesden, stationer, troubled or attracted, an outsider though, who had passed and repassed it three or four times between the hours of eight and nine, p.m., and at half-past nine had backed into the recess of Mr. Wesden's doorway. A small outsider, of uncertain age—a boy, a nondescript, an anything, judging by the pinched white face and unkempt hair; a girl, by the rag of a frock that hung upon her, and from which her legs and feet protruded.

Subject matter of great interest was there for this small watcher—huddled in the doorway, clutching her elbows with her bony fingers, and listening at the keyhole, or varying proceedings now and then by stepping on to the clammy pavement, and looking up, through the fog, at the lighted blinds, once or twice indulging in a flat-footed kind of jig, to keep her feet warm. She was one of few loiterers in Great Suffolk Street that uncomfortable night—men, women, and boys hurried rapidly past, and thinned in number as the night stole on—only a policeman slouched by occasionally, and dismayed her somewhat, judging by her closer proximity to Mr. Wesden's street door, whenever his heavy tread jarred upon her nerves.

When the majority of the shops was closed, when the fog grew denser as the lights went out, and the few stragglers became more phantom-like and grey, quite a regiment of policemen marched down Great Suffolk Street, changing places at certain corners with those officials who had done day-duty, and glad to have done, for that day at least.

The new policeman who crawled upon Mr. Wesden's side of the way, was a sharper man than he who had left off crawling, and gone home at a gallop to his wife and thirteen children; for the new-comer was not deceived by the deep-doorway and the dense fog, but reached forth a hand and touched the figure cowering in the shadows.

A red-faced young man, with a bull neck, was this Suffolk Street official—an abrupt young man, who shook people rather violently by the shoulder, and hurt them.

"Oh!—stash that, please," ejaculated the child, at last; "you hurts!"

"What do you want here?"

"Nothin' partickler. If the young gal inside knows I'm here, she'll send out somethin' prime. That's all. Last thing, afore she goes to bed, she comes and looks, mostly. She's a good 'un."

"Ah! you'd better go home."

"Can't manage to make it up tuppence—and square the last penny with Mother Watts. You know Mother Watts?"

"Ah!"

"Well, she's down upon me, Watts is—so I can't go home."

"You must go somewhere—you can't stop here."

"Lor bless you, this is the comfortablest doorway in the street, if you don't mind, p'leesman. I often turn in here for the night, and some of you fine fellers lets a gal bide, and ain't so down upon her as you are. You're new to this beat."

"Am I, really?" was the ironical rejoinder.

"You used to do Kent Street and stir up Mother Watts. You locked up Mother Watts once—don't you remember?"

"Yes—I remember. Are you going?"

"If you won't let a gal stay, o' course I am. They've got a jolly kick-up here—that gal with the blue frock's birthday—old Wesden's gal, as I just told you about—I wish I was her! Did you ever see her of a Sunday?"

"Not that I know on."

"Just like the little gals at the play—spruce as carrots—and gloves on, and such boots! Fust rate, I can tell you."

"I wouldn't jaw any more, but go home," suggested the policeman.

"All right, master. I say, don't you twig how the fog has got on my chest?"

"Well, you *are* hoarse-ish."

"Spilt my woice yesterday, and made it wus by tryin' it on in Union Street to-day. Gave it up, and bought a haporth of lucifers, and got the boxes in my pocket now. Hard lines to-night, mate."

Familiarity breeds contempt and engenders rebuke—the loquacity of the child offended the official, who drew her from the doorway with a jerk, totally unexpected upon her side, and placed her in the roadway.

"Now be off from here—I've had enough of *you*."

"Werry well—why didn't you say so afore?"

And, without waiting for a reply to her query, the child went down Great Suffolk Street towards the Borough, sullenly and slowly. The policeman watched her vanish in the fog, and resumed his way; he had done his duty to society, and "moved on" one who had insulted it by her helplessness and squalor; there was a woman shrieking denunciations on the pot-man of the public house at the corner—a man who had turned her unceremoniously into the street—let him proceed to business in a new direction.

Twenty steps on his way, and the ill-clad, sharp-visaged girl, stealing back in the fog to the welcome doorway whence he had abruptly expelled her.

"He's not everybody," she ejaculated, screwing herself comfortably into her old quarters, "though he thinks he is. I wonder what they're up to now? Don't I wish it was my buff-day, and somebody had somethink to give me, that's all. Don't I—oh! gemini."

"Hillo!—I beg pardon—I didn't know anyone was hiding here—have I hurt you?" inquired a youth, who, running down Great Suffolk Street at a smart pace, had turned into this doorway, and nearly jammed its occupant to death with the sudden concussion.

"You've done for my lights, young un," was the grave assertion.

"Your—your what?"

"My congreve lights—there's a kiver gone—I heered it scrunch. S'pose you'll pay like a—like a man?"

"I—I'm very sorry, but really I'm rather scarce of pocket-money just now—in fact, I've spent it all," stammered the lad. "You see, it was your fault, hiding here, and playing about here at this time of night, and I was in a hurry, being late."

"There isn't anyone inside who'd stand a ha-penny, is there?" whined the girl; "I'm the gal that's allus about here, you know—I've had nuffin' to eat to-day, and ain't no money for a night's lodging. I'm hard up—wery hard up, upon my soul. I don't remember being so druv since mother died o' the fever—never. And I'm not well—got a sore throat, which the fog touches up—awful."

"I'll—I'll ask my pa'; but I don't think there is anything to give away."

The youth knocked at the door, and presently rushed by the servant who opened it, paying no heed to the remark of—

"Well, you are late, Master Sidney, I must say!"

The door closed again, and Master Sidney—a tall lad of fourteen, with long brown hair, brown eyes, and a white face—tore up the stairs two steps at a time, and dashed with but little ceremony into the dining-room, where the supper was laid by that time, and the juveniles were ranged round the table, large-eyed and hungry.

A shout from the boys assembled there—"Here's Sidney Hinchford;" a reproof from a stiff-backed, white-haired old gentleman in the corner—"Where *have* you been, boy?" a light-haired fairy in white muslin and blue sash darting towards him, crying, "Sidney, Sidney, I thought you were lost!"

"So I have been—lost in the fog—such a mull of it! I'll tell you presently when I've spoken to pa' for a moment. And, oh! Harriet, here's—here's a little brooch I've bought, and with many happy, happy returns of the day from a tiresome playfellow, and—and—*stolen, by Jingo*!"

The hand withdrew itself from the side pocket of his jacket, and was passed over the forehead, the lower jaw dropped, the brown eyes glared round the room, across at the opposite wall, and up at the gas branch—a two-burner of a bronze finger-post pattern,—and then Master Sidney doubled up suddenly and collapsed.

CHAPTER II.

MATTIE.

Mrs. Sarah Jane Watts, better known to society and society's guardians by the cognomen of Mother Watts, kept a lodging-house in Kent Street. They who know where Kent Street, Borough is, and what Kent Street is like by night and day, can readily imagine that the establishment of Mrs. Watts was not a large one, or the prices likely to be high. Mrs. Watts' house, in fact, belonged not to Kent Street proper, but formed No. 2 of a cut-throat-looking court, crossing Kent Street at right angles. Here beds, or shares of beds, or shelves arranged horizontally under beds, were let out at twopence per head, or three-halfpence without the blankets, which were marked, "Stop Thief!"

Whether Mrs. Watts did badly with her business, or whether business prospered with her, it was difficult to determine by the landlady's external appearance, Mrs. W. being ever in rags, ever full of complaints and—drink. "Times" were always hard with her—the police were hard with her—her Kent Street contemporaries were hard with her—didn't treat her fair, undersold her, put more in a bed and charged less—"split upon her when things weren't on the square. Kent Street wasn't what it was when she was a gal!"

People constantly breathing the same atmosphere may notice a change in the "surroundings," but to common observers, or prying people paying occasional visits to this place, Kent Street seems ever the same—an eye-sore to public gaze, a satire on parish cleanliness and care, a disgrace to parish authorities in general, and landlords and ground landlords in particular.

Ever to common eyes the same appearances in Kent Street. The bustle of a cheap trade in its shops; the knots of thieves and loose-livers at every narrow turning; the murmurs of unseen disputants, in the true London vernacular, welling from dark entries and up-stairs rooms; the shoals of children, hatless, shoeless, almost garmentless—all a medley of sights and sounds, increasing towards night-fall, when Kent Street is full of horror, and lives and purses are not safe there.

It is eleven in the evening of the same day, in which our story opens, and Mrs. Sarah Jane Watts, baggy as regards costume, and unsteady as regards her legs, was standing in the doorway of her domicile, inspecting, by the light of the candle in her hand, a trinket of some kind, which had been proffered her by a smaller mortal, infinitely more ragged than herself.

"You got it honestly—I takes your word for it—you allers was a gal who spoke the truth, I will say that for you—it's a sham affair, and brassy as a knocker—say eightpence?"

"It's really gold, Mrs. Watts—it's worth a heap of money."

"It's the brassiest thing that ever I clapped eyes on—say eightpence and a bit of supper?"

"What sort o' supper?"

"Hot supper—tripe and inguns—as much as you can pad with."

"It's worth a sight more, if it's gold."

"I'll ask Simes—go up-stairs and wait a minit'—Simes'll tell us if it's gold, and praps stand more for it. I don't want the thing—I don't think it's safe to keep, myself; and if you've prigged it, Mattie, why, you'd better let it go."

"Very well."

Mattie—the girl whom we have watched in the dark entry of Mr. Wesden's door, wearied out with Mrs. Watts' loquacity, or overpowered by her arguments, went up-stairs into a room on the first floor. A long, low-ceilinged room, containing three beds, and each bed containing four women and a few supplementary children, one affected with a whooping-cough that was evidently fast racking it to death. This was the feminine dormitory of Mrs. Watts—a place well known to London women in search of a night's rest, Southwark way—a place for the ballad singer who had twopence to spend, or a soul above the workhouse; for the beggar-women who had whined about the streets all day; for the tramps passing from Surrey to Essex, and taking London *en route*; for women of all callings, who were deplorably poor, idle or vicious—it mattered not, so that they paid Mrs. Watts her claim upon them.

Mattie sat down by the fire, and began shivering with more violence than had characterized her in the cold and fog. The disturbed shadow, flung by the fire-light—the only light there—on the wall, shivered and danced grotesquely in the rear. No one took notice of the new-comer—although more than one woman lay awake in the background. A wrinkled hag, reposing with her basket of stay-laces under her head for security's sake, winked and blinked at her for a while, and then went off into a disjointed snore—the young mother with the sick child, sat up in her share of the bed, and rocked the coughing infant backwards and forwards, till her neighbour, with an oath, swore at her for letting the cold in; then all was as Mattie had found it upon entering.

Presently Mrs. Watts returned, candle in hand, smelling more aromatically of something hot and strong than ever.

"Simes says it's brass, and worth eightpence, and here's the money. Strike me dead, if he said more than eightpence, there!—strike him blind, if he'll get a farden out of it!"

"Where's the money?"

"Here's fippence—tuppence for to-night, and a penny you owe me, that makes eightpence; and as for supper, why, I'll keep my word—no one can ever say of Mother Watts that she didn't keep her word in anythink she undertooked."

"I—I don't care so much about supper as I did—ain't I just husky? No singing to-morrow, mother."

"Only singing small," was the rejoinder with a grunt at her own wit; "you'd do better picking up brooches—you was allers clever with your fingers, mind you. I only wish I'd been 'arf as sharp when I was young."

"I—I only wish I hadn't—found the thing," commented the girl, sorrowfully.

"Well, I'm blest!"

Mrs. Watts was taking off the lid of her saucepan, and probing the contents with a fork.

"Fippence isn't a fortun, and the young chap gave me a ha-penny once when I was singing in Suffolk Street—I didn't mean it, somehow—I said I never would again! Don't you remember when mother died here, how she went on just at the last as to what was to become o' me; and didn't I say I'd grow up good, and stick to singing and begging, and all that *fun*—or go to the workus—or anythink?"

"Ah! your mother was a fine 'un to go on sometimes."

"And then I——"

"Now, I don't want to hear anythink about your goings on—I don't know where you found that brassy brooch—I don't want to know—Simes don't want to know! We takes your word for it, that it was come by proper, and the less you say about it, the better; and the sooner you turns into bed, if you don't want no supper, the better too."

"I don't see a good twopen'orth over there," commented Mattie; "they're as full as ever they can stick."

"Take the rug, gal, and have it all to yourself, here by the fire."

"Well, it's not so bad. I say—you know old Wesden?"

"What, in Suffolk Street?—well."

"He's got a party to-night—I have been a listening to the music—they've been dancing and all manner. And laughing—my eye! they just have been a-laughing, Mother Watts—I've been laughing myself to hear 'em."

"Um," was the unsympathetic response.

"It's a buff-day—Wesden's gal's buff-day. You know Wesden's gal—proud of herself rather, and holds her head up in furst-rate style, as well she may with such a shop as her father's got in Suffolk Street, and good and pretty as she is, Lor bless her! I s'pose old Wesden's worth pounds and pounds now?"

"Hundreds."

"Hundreds and hundreds of pounds," commented Mattie, coiling herself in the rug upon the floor; "ah! I s'pose so. I often thinks, do you know, I should like to be Wesden's little gal—what a lucky thing it'd be to be turned somehow into Wesden's little gal, just at Christmas time, when fairies are about."

"What!"

"Real fairies, on course—not the gals with the legs in the pantermines. If there was any real fairies on course too, but I'm too knowing to b'lieve that. But if there was, I'd say, please turn me into Wesden's little gal, and give me the big doll by the parler door, and dress me like a lady in a blue meriner."

"Well, you are going on nicely about Wesden's gal. That was allus your fault, Mattie—such a gal to jaw, jaw, jaw—such a clapper, clapper, clapper about everythink and everybody."

"I was just a-thinking that I *was* going it rather, but I ain't a bit sleepy, and I thought you wouldn't mind me while you was having your supper, and my throat's so awful sore, and you ain't so sharp quite, as you are sometimes. Do you know what I'd do, if I was a boy?"

"How should I know?"

"Go to sea—get away from here, and grow up 'spectable. I wouldn't stop in Kent Street—I hate Kent Street—I'd walk into the country—oh! ever so far—until I came to the sea, and then I'd find a ship and turn sailor."

"Lookee here, you young drab," cried the stay-lace woman, suddenly opening her eyes, and shrieking out in a shrill falsetto, "I'll turn out and skin you, if you can't keep that tongue still. What am I here for?—what did I pay tuppence for?—isn't that cussed coughing baby enough row at a time?"

"If you've got anythink to say aginst my baby," said a husky voice in the next bed, "say it out to his mother, and mind your cat's head while you say it, you disagreeable baggage!"

"Well, the likes of that!"

"And the likes of you, for that matter—don't give me any more of your sarse, or I'll——"

A tapping on the door with a stick diverted the general attention.

"Who's there?"

"Only me, Mrs. Watts."

"Oh! *only* you," was the response; "come in, will yer? I've no need to lock myself in, while I hide the swag away. *Now*, what's the matter?"

The door was opened, and enter a policeman, a man in private clothes, with a billycock hat and a walking-stick, accompanied by a pale-faced, long-haired youth, of fourteen years of age.

"Nothing particular the matter—only something lost as usual, Mrs. Watts," said the man in private dress, politely. "Where's Mattie to-night?"

"There she is. She's been in all the evening with a bad throat."

"Poor girl—throats *is* bad at this time of the year."

The speaker looked at the lad at his side, after giving the first turn backward to the rug.

"Is this the girl?"

The policeman took the candle from the table, and held the light close to the girl's face—white, pinched, and haggard, with black eyes full of horror.

"Don't say it's me, please," she gasped, in a low voice; "I'm the gal that sings in Suffolk Street on a Saturday night, and they gives wittles to at Wesden's. It isn't me."

Mattie had intended to brave it out at first, to have remained stolid, sullen, and defiant, after the manners of her class; but she felt ill and nervous, and the shadow of the prison-house loomed before her and made her heart sink. Prison was a comfortable place in its way, but she had never taken to it—one turn at it had been enough for her. If it had been a policeman, or old Wesden, or anybody but this boy three years her senior in age, many years her junior in knowledge of the world, she would have been phlegmatic to the last; but this boy had been kind to her twice in life—once on Christmas-eve, and once on a Saturday night before that, and she gave way somewhat, partly from her new and unaccountable weakness, partly because it was not a very stern face that looked down into hers.

"That's her, sure enough—eh, young gentleman?" remarked the police officer in private clothes.

There was another pause—the girl's face blanched still more, and the look in her eyes became even more intense and eager; the boy glanced over his shoulder at the servants of the law.

"No—this isn't the girl. Oh! no."

"Are you quite certain? Stand up, Mattie."

Mattie turned out of her rug and stood up, erect and motionless, with her hands to her side, and her sharp black eyes still on Master Hinchford.

"Oh! no, policeman. Ever so much taller!"

"Then we're on the wrong scent it seems, and you'd better go home and leave it to us. Good night, Mrs. Watts."

"Good night," was the muttered response.

Policeman, detective, and Master Hinchford went down the stairs to the court, out of the court into Kent Street, black and noisome—a turgid current, that wore only a semblance of stillness at hours more late than that.

"We'll let you know in the morning if there's any clue," said the detective. "Jem," to the policeman, "see this lad out of Kent Street."

"All right. I think I'd try old Simes for the brooch."

"I'll drop on him presently. Good night, Jem."

"Good night."

The boy and policeman went to the end of Kent Street together, then the boy bade the policeman good night, ran across the road, recrossed in the fog a little lower down, and edged his way round St. George's Church into the old objectionable thoroughfare. A few minutes afterwards, he walked cautiously into the up-stairs room of Mrs. Watts, startling that good lady at her late tripe supper very considerably.

"Hollo! young gemman, what's up now?"

Mattie, who had been crouching before the fire, shrank towards it more, with her hands spread out to the blaze. She looked over her shoulder at the door, anticipating his two unwelcome companions to follow in his wake.

"Look here, Mattie," said he, in a very cool and business-like manner, "fair's fair, you know. I've let you off in a handsome manner, but I'm not going to lose the brooch. If it had been a trumpery brooch, I shouldn't have cared so much."

"Was it real gold?"

"A real gold heart. I gave twelve and sixpence for it—I've been saving up for it ever since last April."

"I'll get it—I'll try and get it," said Mattie; "I haven't it myself now—it's been passed on. Upon my soul, I'll try my hardest to get it back, see if I don't."

"We'll all try our werry hardest, sir," remarked Mrs. Watts, blandly.

"Ah! I daresay you will," said the boy, dubiously; "p'raps it had been better if I'd told the truth—my pa always says 'Stick to the truth, Sidney;' but you did look such a poor body to lock up, that I told a lie for once. And who would have thought that you were a regular thief, Mattie!"

"I'm not a reg'lar—I don't like thieving—I've only thove when I've been werry—werry—hard druv; and I wasn't thinking of thieving, ony of getting warm, when you came bump aginst me in the doorway. I meant to have knocked and asked for a scrap to eat after awhile, when they'd all got good-tempered over the beer and things. I'll bring the brooch—I'll get it back—leave it to me, Master Hinchford."

"How did you know my name?"

"Oh! I know everybody about here—everybody at your place, 'specially. Old Wesden and his gal in the blue meriner—and you, and your father with the red face and the white mustache and hair—and the servant, and the boy who takes the papers out, and is allus dropping them out of the oil-skin kiver, and everybody. I'll bring the brooch, because you let me off. Trust me," she repeated again.

"Well, I'll trust you. Fair play, mind."

"And now, cut out of this—it isn't quite a safe place for you, and the people can't sleep if you talk, and you may catch the whooping cough——"

"And you'll bring the brooch back? It's a bargain between us, Mattie."

"It's all right."

The youth re-echoed "all right," and went down-stairs, watched from the dark landing by the girl who had robbed him. After a while the girl closed the door and followed slowly down-stairs also. She was going in search of old Simes.

CHAPTER III.

LODGERS.

"Depend upon it, Sidney, you'll never set eyes on that brooch again."

"I'm not so sure about that," was the half-confident reply.

"And depend upon it, you don't deserve to see it, boy—and that I for one shall be glad if it never turns up."

"Pa!—you really can't mean it."

"You told a lie about it, Sidney, and though you saved the girl from prison, yet it was a big, black lie all the same; and if luck follows it, why it's clean against the Bible."

"The girl looked so pitifully at me, you see—and I did think she might give the brooch back, out of gratitude."

"Gratitude in a young thief out of Kent Street?" laughed the father; "well, it's a lesson in life to you, boy, and, after all, it only cost twelve and sixpence."

"Ah!" sighed Sidney, "it was a long pull."

"You'll have learned by this that a lie never prospers—that in the long run it confronts you again when least expected, to make your cheek burn with your own baseness. I wonder now," gravely surveying his son, "whether you would have let that girl off, if there had been no hope of the brooch coming to light."

The boy hesitated—then looked full at his sire.

"Well—I think I should."

"I think you told a lie for twelve and sixpence—the devil got a bargain from a Hinchford."

"You're rather hard upon me, pa," complained the boy, "and it wasn't for twelve and sixpence, because I never got the brooch back; and if I ever tell another lie, may I never see twelve and sixpence of my own again. There!"

"Bravo, Sid!—that's a promise I'm glad to have wormed out of you, somehow. And yet—ye gods!—what a promise!"

"I'll keep it—see if I don't," said Master Sidney, with his lips compressed, and his cheeks a little flushed.

The father shook his head slowly.

"You are going into business—you will be a business man,—presently a City man—one who will drive hard bargains, make hard bargains, and have to fight his way through a hundred thousand liars. In the pursuit of money—above all, in the scraping together of that fugitive article, you must lie, or let a good chance go by to turn an honest penny. I can't expect you *much* better than other men, Sid."

"I wonder whether uncle lied much before——"

"He lied as little as he could, I daresay," quickly interrupted the father, "but he became a rich man, and he rose from City trading. But I told you once before—I think I have told you more than once—that I never wish to hear that uncle's name."

"Yes, but I had forgotten it for the moment—speaking of money-making, and City men, threw me a little off my guard."

"Yes, yes, I saw that, my boy—drop the curtain over the old grievance, and shut the past away from you and me. I don't complain—I'm happy enough—a little contents me. In the future, with a son to love and be proud of, I see the old man's happiest days!"

"We'll try our best, sir, to make them so," exclaimed the boy.

"The Hinchfords are a buoyant race, and are not to be always kept down. I never heard of more than one of us, a poor man in the same generation; the Hinchfords have intelligence, perseverance, and pluck, and they make their way in the world. If I have been unlucky in my time, and have dropped down to a lodging in Great Suffolk Street, I see the next on the list," laying his hand lightly on his boy's shoulder, "making his way to the higher ground, God willing."

"I haven't made much way yet," remarked the son, checking quietly the ambitious dreaming of the father. "I have only left school two months, and an office-boy in Hippen's firm is not a very great affair, after all."

"It's a step forward—don't grumble—you'll push your way—you're a Hinchford."

"I'll do my best—I never was afraid of work."

"No—rather too fond of it, I fear. Sometimes I think there is no occasion to pore, pore, pore over those books of an evening, studying a lot of dry works, which can never be of service to a City man."

"I should like to be *precious* clever!" was the boy's exclamation.

The father laughed, and added, with more satire than the boy detected—

"The precious clever ones seek out-of-the-way roads to fortune, and miss them—die in the workhouse, occasionally. It is only respectable mediocrity that jogs on to independence."

This strange dialogue between father and son occurred in the first-floor of the little stationer's shop in Great Suffolk Street. Father and son had lodged there eight years at least; Mrs. Hinchford, a delicate woman, several years her husband's junior, had died there—the place was home to the stiff-backed, white-haired man, who had prophesied a rise in life for his son. Eight or nine years ago, the three Hinchfords had walked into Mr. Wesden's shop, and looked at the apartments that had been announced to be let from the front pane of the first-floor windows; had, after a little whispering together, decided on the rooms, and had never left them since, the wife excepted, who had died with her husband's hand in hers, praying for her boy's future. The Hinchfords had settled as firmly to those rooms on the first-floor, as Mr. Wesden, stationer, had settled to Great Suffolk Street in ages remote. The rent was low, the place was handy for Mr. Hinchford, who was clerk and book-keeper to a large builders, Southwark Bridge Road way; the attendance was not a matter of trouble to the Hinchfords, and the landlord and his wife were unobtrusive people, and preferred the lodgers rent to their society.

For three years and a half the Hinchfords and Wesdens had only exchanged good mornings in their meetings on the stairs—the Wesdens were humble, taciturn folk, and the Hinchfords proud and stand-offish. After that period Mrs. Hinchford fell ill, and Mrs. Wesden became of service to her; helped, at last, to nurse her, and keep her company during the long hours of her husband's absence at business, even to take care of her noisy boy down-stairs, when his boisterousness in the holidays made his presence—much as the mother loved him—unbearable. The Wesdens were kind to the Hinchfords, and Mr. Hinchford, a man to be touched by true sympathy, unbent at that time. He was a proud man, but a sensible one, and he never forgot a kindness proffered him. He had belonged to a higher estate once, and, dropping suddenly to a lower, he had brought his old notions with him, to render him wretched and uneasy. He had thought himself above those Wesdens—petty hucksters, as they were—until the time when Mrs. Wesden became a kind nurse to his wife, almost a mother to his boy; and then he felt his own inferiority to a something in them, or belonging to them, and was for ever after that intensely grateful.

When Mrs. Hinchford died, and the lonely man had got over his first grief, he sought Mr. Wesden's company more often, smoked a friendly pipe with him in the back parlour now and then—begged to do so, for refuge from that solitary drawing-room up-stairs, filled with such sad memories as it was then. Hinchford and Wesden did not talk much, the latter was not fond of talking; and they were odd meetings enough, either in the parlour, or in the up-stairs room, as business necessitated.

They exchanged a few words about the weather, and the latest news in the papers, and then subsided into their tobacco-smoke till it was time to say good night; but Wesden was company for Hinchford in his trouble, and when time rendered the trouble less acute, each had fallen into the habit of smoking a pipe together once or twice a week, and did not care to break it.

In the parlour meetings, Mrs. Wesden would bring her spare form and pinched countenance between them, and would sit darning socks and saying little to relieve the monotony—unless the little girl were sitting up late, and her vivacity required attention or reprimand. They were quiet evenings with a vengeance, and Hinchford took his cue from the couple who managed business in Great Suffolk Street—and managed it well, for they minded their own, and were not disturbed by other people's.

Whilst we are looking back—taking a passing glimpse over our shoulder at the bygones—we may as well add, that the Wesdens were naturally quiet people, and did not put on company-manners for Mr. Hinchford in particular. Thirty years ago they had married and opened shop in Great Suffolk Street; struggled for a living without making a fuss about it; lived frugally, pinched themselves in many ways which the world never knew anything about; surmounted the first obstacles in their way, and then, in the same quiet manner, saved a little money, then a little more, and then, as if by habit, continued saving, maintaining the same appearance in themselves, and the same quaint stolidity towards their neighbours. They had even borne their family troubles quietly, losing three children out of four without any great demonstration of grief—keeping their lamentations for after-business hours, and their inflexible faces for their curious neighbours, to whom they seldom spoke, and from whom they chose no friends. They were a couple contented with themselves and their position in society,—a trifle too frugal, if not near—staid, jogtrot, business people of week days, church-goers who patronized free seats for economy's sake on Sundays.

Once a year the Wesdens launched out—celebrating, in the month of January, the natal day of the bright-faced girl in whom so much love was centred, for whom they were working steadily and persistently still. They had a juvenile party on that day always, and Harriet's school friends came in shoals to the feast, and Mr. Wesden presented his compliments to Mr. Hinchford, and begged the favour of borrowing the drawing-room for one night, and hoped also to have the honour of Mr. Hinchford's company, and Master Hinchford's company, on that occasion—all of which being responded to in the affirmative, affairs went off, as a rule, satisfactorily, until that momentous night in January, when Master Sidney Hinchford lost his brooch.

This incident altered many things, and led to many things undreamed of by the characters yet but in outline in these pages; without it we should not have sat down to tell the history of these people—bound up so inextricably with that poor wanderer of the streets whom we have heard called Mattie.

CHAPTER IV.

MR. HINCHFORD'S EXPERIMENT.

The middle of March; six weeks since the robbery of Master Hinchfords' gold heart; a wet night in lieu of a foggy one; a cold wind sweeping down the street and dashing the rain all manner of ways; pattens and clogs clicking and shuffling about the pavement of Great Suffolk Street; the stationery shop open, and Mr. Wesden at seven o'clock sitting behind the counter waiting patiently for customers.

Being a wet night, and customers likely to be scarce in consequence, Mr. Wesden had carefully turned out one gas burner and lowered the two others in the window to imperceptible glimmers of a despondent character, and then taken his seat behind the counter ready for any amount of business that might turn up between seven and half-past nine p.m. The gas was burning more brightly in the back parlour, through the closed glass door of which Mrs. Wesden was cutting out shirts, and Miss Wesden learning, or feigning to learn, her school lessons for the morrow.

Mr. Wesden was devoting his mind purely to business; in his shop he never read a book, or looked at a newspaper, but waited for customers, always in one position, with his head slightly bent forwards, and his hands clutching his knees. In that position the largest order had not the power to stagger him—the smallest order could not take him off his guard. He bent his mind to business—he was "on duty" for the evening.

Mr. Wesden was a short, spare man, with a narrow chest, a wrinkled face, a sharp nose, and a sandy head of hair—a man whose clothes were shabby, and ill fitted him, the latter not to be wondered at, Mrs. Wesden being the tailor, and making everything at home. This saved money, and satisfied Mr. Wesden, who cared not for appearances, had a soul above the fashion, and a faith in his wife's judgment. In the old days Mrs. Wesden was forced to turn tailor and trouser-maker, or see her husband without trousers at all; tailoring had become a habit since then, and agreed with her—it saved money still, and economy was ever a virtue with this frugal pair.

Mr. Wesden in his shop-suit then—that was his shabbiest suit, and exceedingly shabby it was—sat and waited for customers. He waited patiently; to those who strayed in for sheets of note-paper, books to read, shirt-buttons, tapes, or beads, he was very attentive, settling the demands with promptitude and despatch, saying little save "a wet evening," and not to be led into a divergence about a hundred matters foreign to business, until the articles were paid for, and the money in his till. Then, if a few loquacious customers *would* gossip about the times, he condescended to listen, regarding them from his meaningless grey eyes, and responding in monosyllables, when occasion or politeness required some kind of answer. But he was always glad to see their faces turned towards the door—they wearied him very much, these people, and it was odd they could not take away the articles they had purchased, and go home in quietness.

To people in the streets who, caught by some attraction in his window, stopped and looked thereat, he was watchful from behind his counter—speculating as to whether they were probable purchasers, or had felonious designs. He was a suspicious man to a certain extent as well as a careful one, and no one lingered at his window without becoming an object of interest from behind the tobacco-jars and penny numbers. On this evening a haggard white face—whether a girl or woman's he could not make out for the mist on the window-panes—had appeared several times before the shop-window, and looked in, over the beads, and tapes, and through packets of paper, *at him*. Not interested at anything for sale, but keeping an eye on him, he felt assured.

He had a bill in the window—"A BOY WANTED"—and if it had been a boy's face flitting about in the rain there, he should not have been so full of doubts as to the object with which he was watched; but there was a battered bonnet on the head of the watcher, and therefore no room for speculation concerning sex, at least.

After an hour's fugitive dodging, Mattie—for it was she—came at a slow rate into the shop. She walked forwards very feebly, and took a firm grip of the counter to steady herself.

Mr. Wesden critically surveyed her from his post of observation; she did not speak, but she kept her black eyes directed to the face in front of her.

"Well—what do you want, Mattie?" asked Mr. Wesden, finally.

"Nothin'—that is to buy."

"Ah! then we've nothing to give away for you any more."

"I want to speak to Master Hinchford," said Mattie; "I've come about the brooch."

"Not brought it back!" exclaimed Mr. Wesden, roused out of his apathetic demeanour by this assertion.

"I wish I had—no, I on'y want to see him."

Mr. Wesden called to his wife, and delivered Mattie's request through the glass, keeping one eye on the new comer all the while. Mrs. Wesden sent her daughter up-stairs with the message, and presently from a side door opening into the shop Miss Wesden made her appearance.

"If you please, will you walk up-stairs?"

Harriet Wesden spoke very kindly, and edged away from Mattie as she advanced—Mattie was the girl who had stolen the brooch, a strange creature from an uncivilized world, and the stationer's little daughter was afraid of her old pensioner.

The girl from the streets stared at Harriet Wesden in her turn, looked very intently at her warm dress and white pinafore, and then looked back at Mr. Wesden.

"May I go up, sir?"

"I don't see why they can't come down here," he grumbled, "but you must go up if they want to see you. Stop here, Harriet, and call Ann—you might catch something, girl."

Ann was called, and presently a broad-faced, red-armed girl made her appearance.

"Show a light to this girl up-stairs, Ann."

"This girl—here?"

"Yes—that girl there."

"Oh! lawks—so *you've* turned up agin."

Mattie did not answer—she seemed very weak and ill, and not inclined to waste words foreign to her motive in appearing there. She followed the servant up-stairs, pausing on the first landing to take breath.

"What's the matter with you—ain't you well?" asked the servant-maid.

"No, I ain't—I'm just the tother thing."

"Been ill?"

"Scarlet fever—that's all."

"Oh! lor a mussy on us!—keep further off! I can't bide fevers. We shall all be as red as lobsters in the morning."

"It ain't catching now—Mother Watts didn't catch it—I wish she had!"

"Will you go up-stairs now?"

"Let's get a breath—I ain't so strong as I used to be—now then."

Up the next flight, to the door of the first-floor front, where Sidney Hinchford, pale with suspense, was standing.

"Have you got it?—have you got it, Mattie?"

"No—I ain't got nothin'."

"'Cept a fever, Master Sidney—tell your father to look out."

A thin, large-veined hand protruded from the door, and dragged Master Hinchford suddenly backwards into the room; a tall, military-looking old gentleman, with white hair and white moustache, the instant afterwards occupied the place, and looked down sternly at the small intruder.

"Keep where you are—I didn't know you had a fever, girl. Ann Packet, put the light on the bracket. That will do."

Ann Packet set the chamber candlestick on a little bracket outside the drawing-room, drew her clothes tightly round her limbs, and keeping close to the wall, scuttled past the girl, whom fever had sorely stricken lately. Mattie dropped on to the stairs, placed her elbows on her knees, took her chin between her claw-like hands, and stared up at Mr. Hinchford.

"I don't think you can catch anythin' from me, guv'nor."

Governor looked down at Mattie, and reddened a little.

"I'm not afraid of fever—it's only the boy I'm thinking about. Sidney," he called.

"Yes, pa."

"You can hear, if I leave the door open. Now, girl," addressing the diminutive figure on the stairs, "if you haven't brought the brooch, what was the good of coming here?"

"To let you know I tried—that's all. I thought that all you might think that I'd stuck to it, you see. But I did try my hardest to get it back—because the young gent let me off when the bobbies would have walked me to quod. Lor bless you, sir, I'm not a reg'lar!"

"A what?"

"A reg'lar thief, sir. They've been trying hard to make me—Mother Watts and old Simes, and the rest—but it don't do. I was locked up once afore mother died, and mother was sorry—awful sorry, for *her*—you should have just heard her go on, when I come out agin. Oh! no, I'm not a reg'lar—I sings about the street for ha'pence, and goes to fairs, and begs—and so on, but I don't take things werry often. I'm a stray, sir!"

"Ah!—God help you!" murmured the old gentleman.

"I never had no father—and mother's dead now. I'm 'bliged to shift for myself. And oh! I just was hard up when I tooked the brooch."

"And what became of it?"

"Old Simes stuck to it, sir. I went to him on the werry night after I had seen Master Hinchford, and he said he'd sold it for tenpence, but he'd try and get it back for me, which he never did, sir—never."

"No—I suppose not," was the dry response.

"And the next day I caught the fever, and got in the workus, somehow; and when I came back to Kent Street, last week that was, old Simes had seen nothin' more of the brooch, and Mother Watts had forgot all about it—so she said!" was the disparaging comment.

"And you came hither to tell us all this?"

"Yes—I thought you'd like to know I *did* try, and that they were too deep for me. My eye! they just are deep, those two!"

"Why didn't you stay in the workhouse?"

"Can't bide the workus, sir—they drop upon you too much. It's the wust place going, sir, and no one takes to it."

"You're an odd girl."

Mr. Hinchford leaned his back against the door-post, and surveyed the ragged and forlorn girl on the lower stair. He was perplexed with this child, and her wistful eyes—keen and glittering as steel—made him feel uncomfortable. Here was a mystery—a something unaccountable, and he could not probe to its depths, or tell which was false and which was genuine in the character of this motherless girl before him. He had prided himself all his life in being a judge of character—a man of observation, who saw the flaw in the diamond—the real face behind the paint, varnish, and pasteboard. He had judged his own brother in times past—he had mixed much with the world, and gleaned much from hard experience thereof, and yet a child like this disturbed him. He fancied that he could read a struggle for something better and more pure in Mattie's life, and that Fate was against her and drawing her back to the shadows from which she, as if by a noble instinct, was endeavouring to emerge.

He felt curious concerning her.

"What do you intend to do now?"

"Lor, sir, I don't know. It depends upon what turns up."

"You will not thieve any more?"

"Not if I can help it—but if I can't help it, sir, I must go to school at Simes's. He teaches lots of gals to get a living!"

Mr. Hinchford shuddered. There was a pause, during which the head of Master Hinchford peered through the door to note how affairs were progressing. The father detected the movement, and when the head was hastily withdrawn, he drew the door still closer, and retained a grip of the handle for precaution's sake.

"You don't know what your next step will be? You'll try to live honestly, you say?"

"I'll try the ingun dodge. You get's through a heap of inguns at a ha'penny a lot, if the perlice will ony let you be."

"And your stock in trade?"

"What's that?"

"How will you begin? Where are the onions to come from?"

"I shall sing for them to-morrow—my woice is comin' round a bit, Mother Watts says."

Mr. Hinchford pulled at his long white moustache—the girl's confidence and coolness induced him to linger there—something in his own heart led him to continue the conversation. He was a philosopher, a student of human nature, and this was a singular specimen before him.

"What could you live and keep honest upon?"

"Tuppence a day in summer—fourpence in winter. Summer a gal can sleep anywhere—there's some prime places in the Borough Market, and lots o' railway arches, Dockhead way; but it nips you awful hard when the frost's on."

"Well—here's sixpence to set up in business with, Mattie—and as long as you can show me an honest front, and can come here every Saturday night and say, 'I've been honest all the week,' why, I'll stand the same amount."

Mattie's eyes sparkled at this rise in life.

"I'll borrow a basket, and buy some inguns to-morrow. P'raps *you* buy inguns sometimes, and old—Mr. Wesden down-stairs, too. Yes, sir, it's the connexion that budges one up!" she said, with the gravity of an old woman.

"I see. I'll speak to Mr. Wesden about his custom, Mattie. You can go now."

"Thankee, sir."

She rose to her feet, went a few steps down-stairs, paused, and looked back.

"What is it, Mattie?"

"I hope the young gen'leman isn't a fretting much about his *broach*."

"Here, young gentleman," called the father, "do you hear that?"

Master Hinchford laughed from within.

"Oh, no!—I don't fret."

"P'raps some day I shall have saved up enuf to pay him back. That's a *rum* idea, isn't it, sir?"

"Not a bad one, Mattie. Think it over."

"Yes, sir."

Mattie departed, and Mr. Hinchford returned to the sitting-room. Master Hinchford, buried in books, was sitting at the centre table.

"Are you going at figures to-night?"

"Just for a little while, I think."

"You'll ruin your eyes—I've said so fifty times."

"Better have weak eyes than weak brains, sir."

"Not the general idea, lad."

After a while, and when Master Hinchford was scratching away with his pen, the father said—

"You don't say anything about Mattie."

"I think it was very kind of you," said the youth; "and I think—somehow—that Mattie will be grateful."

"Pooh! pooh!" remarked the father, "you'll never make a first-rate city man, if you believe in gratitude. Look at the world sternly, boy. Put not your trust in anything turning out the real and genuine article—work everything by figures."

Master Hinchford looked at his sire, as though he scarcely understood him.

"I must bring you up to understand human nature, Sid—what a bad article it is—plated with a material that soon wears off, if rubbed smartly. Human nature is everywhere the same, and if you be only on your guard, you may take advantage of it, instead of letting it take advantage of you. Now, this girl is a specimen, which, at my own expense, we will experimentalize upon. In that stray, my boy, you shall see the natural baseness of mankind—or girl-kind."

"Don't you think that she'll come again?"

"For the sixpence, to be sure! Every Saturday night, with a long story of how honest she has been all the week. Here we shall see a girl, who, by her own statement, and with a struggle, can keep honest now—note the effect of indiscriminate alms-giving."

"Of rewarding a girl for stealing my brooch, pa."

"Ah!—exactly. Some people who didn't understand me, would set me down for a weak-minded old fool. In studying human nature, one must act oddly with odd specimens. And this girl—who came to tell us she had not brought the brooch back—I am just a little—curious—concerning!"

CHAPTER V.

SET UP IN BUSINESS.

I am afraid that the reader will be very much disgusted with us as story-tellers, when we inform him that all these details are but preliminary to our story proper—a kind of prologue in six chapters to the comedy, melodrama or tragedy—which?—that the curtain will rise upon in our next book. Still they are details, without which our characters, and their true positions on our stage, would not have been clearly defined; and in the uphill struggles of our stray, perhaps some student of human nature, like Mr. Hinchford, may take some little interest.

For they were real uphill struggles to better herself, and, therefore, worthy of notice. Remarking them, and knowing their genuineness, it has struck us that even from these crude materials a kind of heroine might be fashioned—not the heroine of a high-class book—that is, a "book for the Boudoir"—but of a book that will at least attempt to draw a certain phase of life as plainly as it passed the writer's eyes once.

Let us, ere we *begin* our story, then, speak of this Mattie a little more—this girl, who was not a "reg'lar"—who had never been brought up to "the profession"—who was merely a Stray! Let us even watch her in her new vocation—set up in life with Mr. Hinchford's sixpence—and note by what strange accident it changed the tenor of *her* life; and at least set her above the angry dash of those waves which, day after day, engulph so many.

All that we know of Mattie, all that Mattie knew of herself, the reader is fully acquainted with. Mattie's mother, a beggar, a tramp, occasionally a thief, died in a low lodging-house, and, with some flash of the better instincts at the last, begged her child to keep good, *if she could.* And the girl, by nature impressionable, only by the force of circumstance callous and cunning, tried to subsist on the streets without filching her neighbours' goods—wavered in her best intentions, as well she might, when the world was extra vigorous with her—grew more worldly with the world's hardness, and stole now and then for bread, when there was no bread offered her; made friends with young thieves—"reg'lars"—of both sexes; constituted them her playmates, and rehearsed with them little dramas of successful peculation; fell into bad hands—receivers of stolen goods, and owners of dens where thieves nightly congregated; regarded the police as natural enemies, the streets as home, and those who filled them as men and women to be imposed upon, to be whined out of money by a beggar's plaint, amused out of it by a song in a shrill falsetto, tricked out of it by a quick hand in the depths of their pockets. Still Mattie never became a "reg'lar;" she earned money enough "to keep life in her"—she had become inured to the streets, and had a fear, a very uncommon one in girls of her age and mode of living, of the police-station and the magistrate. Possibly her voice saved her; she had sung duets with her mother before death had stepped between them, and she sold ballads on her own account when the world was all before her where to choose. She was a girl, too, whom a little contented; one who could live on a little, and make shift—terrible shift—when luck run against her; above all, her tempters, the Watts, Simes', and others, festering amongst the Kent Street courts, were cruel and hard with her, and she kept out of their way so long as it was possible.

Given the same monotony of existence for a few more years, and Mattie would have become a tramp perhaps, oscillating from fair to fair, race-course to race-course, losing true feeling, modesty, heart and soul, at every step. She had already tried the fairs within ten miles—the races at Hampton and Epsom, &c., and had earned money at them—she was seeing her way to business next summer, at the time she was interested in one particular house in Great Suffolk Street, Borough.

Mattie was fond of pictures, and therefore partial to Mr. Wesden's shop, where the cheap periodicals and tinsel portraits of celebrated stage-ranters, in impossible positions, were displayed—fond, too, of watching Mr. Wesden's daughter in her perambulations backwards and forwards to a day-school in Trinity Street, and critically surveying her bright dresses, her neat shoes and boots, her hats for week days, and drawn bonnets for Sundays, with a far-off longing, such as a destitute child entertains for one in a comfortable position—such a feeling as we envious children of a larger growth may experience when our big friends flaunt their wealth in our eyes, and talk of their hounds, their horses, and their princely estates.

"Oh! to be only Harriet Wesden," was Mattie's secret wish—to dress like her, look like her, be followed by a mother's anxious eyes down the street; to have a father to see her safely across the broad thoroughfare lying between Great Suffolk Street and school; to go to school, and be taught to read and write and grow up good—what happiness, unattainable and intangible to dream of!

Eugene Sue, I think, tried to show the bright side of Envy, and the good it might effect; and I suppose there are many species of Envy, or else that we do not call things invariably by their right names. Mattie at least envied the stationer's daughter; Miss Wesden was a princess to her, and lived in fairy-land; and in seeing how happy she was, and what good spirits she had, Mattie's own life seemed dark enough; but that other life which Mattie tried to keep aloof from, denser and viler still. Harriet Wesden was the heroine of her story, and in a far-off distant way—never guessed at by its object—

Harriet Wesden was loved, especially after she had begun to notice Mattie's attention to the pictures in the window, and to change them for her sole edification more often than was absolutely necessary.

Mattie was well known in Great Suffolk Street; they knew her at Wesden's—nearly every shopkeeper knew her, and exchanged a word or two with her occasionally—Great Suffolk Street was her *beat*. In health Mattie was a good-tempered, sharp-witted girl—bearing the ills of her life with composure—selling lucifers and singing for a living.

They trusted her in Great Suffolk Street; the poor folk living at the back thereof bought lucifers of her of a Saturday night, and asked how she was getting on—the boys guarding their masters' shop-boards nodded in a patronizing way at her—now and then, a plate of broken victuals was tendered her from some well-to-do shopkeeper, who could afford to part with it, and not miss it either—before her fever, she had had a little "c'nexion," and she set to work to get it up again, when the Hinchford sixpence heaped her basket with onions.

That was the turning-point of Mattie's life; after that, a little woman with an eye to business; a small female costermonger with a large basket before her suspended by a strap—troubled and kept moving on by policemen—but earning her fair modicum of profit; quick with her eyes, ready with her answers, happy as a queen whose business was brisk, and lodging away from Mother Watts and old Simes, whose acquaintance she had quietly dropped.

Mattie still watched Harriet Wesden from a distance; still felt the same strange interest in that girl, one year her senior, growing up so pretty whilst she became so plain and weather-beaten; experiencing still the same attraction for that house in particular; knowing each of its inmates by heart, and feeling, since the brooch defalcation, a part of the history attached to the establishment. When the Wesdens made up their minds to send Harriet to boarding-school, by way of a finish to her education, Mattie learned the news, and was there to see the cab drive off; Mattie even told Ann Packet, servant to the Wesdens, and regular purchaser of Mattie's "green stuff," that she should miss her werry much, and Suffolk Street wouldn't be half Suffolk Street after she was gone—which observation being reported to Mrs. Wesden, directed more attention to the stray from that quarter, and made one more friend at least.

One more—for Mattie had found a friend in the tall, stiff-backed, stern-looking old gentleman of the name of Hinchford. The lodger's philosophy had all gone wrong; his knowledge of human nature had been at fault; his prophecies concerning Mattie's ingratitude had proved fallacious, and her steady application to business had greatly interested him. He was a sterling character, this old gentleman, for he confessed that he had been wrong; and he now held forth Mattie's industry as an example of perseverance in the world to his son, just as in the past he had intended her as a striking proof of the world's ingratitude.

The climax was reached two years after his dialogue with Mattie on the stairs—when Mattie was thirteen years of age, and Master Hinchford sixteen—when Mattie still hawked goods in Suffolk Street—quite a woman of the world, and deeply versed in market prices—one who had not even at that time attained to the dignity of shoes and stockings.

Mr. Wesden, the quiet man of business, was in his shop as usual, when Mattie walked in, basket and all.

Mr. Wesden regarded her gravely, and shook his head. Onions and some sweet herbs had been speculated in that morning, and no further articles were required at that establishment.

"If you please, I don't want you to buy, Mr. Wesden—" said she, "but will you be good enough to send that up to Master Hinchford?"

Mr. Wesden looked at the small, dirty piece of paper in which something was wrapped, and then at Mattie.

"It's honestly come by, sir," said Mattie.

"I never said it wasn't," he responded.

Mattie retired into the street—it was a Saturday night, and there were many customers abroad—she was doing a flourishing trade, when a tall youth caught her by the arm, and dragged her round the corner of the first street.

"Oh! don't pinch my arm so, Master Hinchford."

"What's the twelve and sixpence for, Mattie—not for the—not for the——"

"Yes, the *broach*! I've been a-saving up, and keeping myself down for it, and now it's easy on my mind."

"I won't have it. I've been thinking about it, and I won't have it, Mattie."

"Please do. I've been trying so hard to wipe *that* off. I'm quite well now. I've got the c'nexion all right, and shall save it all up agin, and the winter's arf over, and when Miss Wesden comes back, you can buy her another brooch with it, and nobody disapinted."

The youth laughed, and coloured, and shook his head.

"I won't take twelve and sixpence from you, I tell you. Why, Mattie, you don't know the value of money, or you'd never fling it away like this. Why, it's a fortune to you."

"No—it's been a *weight*—that twelve and six, somehow. I've been a thief until to-night—now it's wiped clean. Don't try to make me a thief agin by giving it on me back. Oh! don't please stop my trade like this!"

"Well, I shall make you out in time, Mattie—*perhaps*."

Master Hinchford pocketed the money, and walked away slowly. Mattie returned to her "c'nexion." Mr. Hinchford sat and philosophized to himself all the evening on the impracticability of arriving at a thorough understanding of human nature, as exemplified in "girl-kind."

CHAPTER VI.

THE END OF THE PROLOGUE.

Hard times set in after that night. The winter was half over, Mattie had said; but the worst half was yet to come, and for that she, with many thousands like her, had made but little preparation. The worst half of the frost of that year set in like a blight upon the London streets, froze the gutters, raised the price of coals, sent provisions up to famine figures, cut off all the garden stuff, and threw such fugitive traders as Mattie completely out of work. Hers became a calling that required capital now; even the greengrocers' shops, Borough way, were scantily stocked—the market itself was not what it used to be when things were flourishing, and oh! the prices that were asked in those times!

Poverty of an ill aspect set in soon after the frost; crime set in soon after poverty—when the workhouses are besieged by hungry claimants for relief, the prisons are always extra full. Suffolk Street, the streets branching thitherwards to Southwark Bridge, the narrow lanes and turnings round the Queen's Bench, in the Borough Road and verging towards Union Street, were all haunted by those phantoms that had set in with the frost—there was danger in the streets as well as famine, and money was hard to earn, and hold when earned! Small shopkeepers with large families closed their shutters and locked themselves in with desolation; men out of work grew desperate—the streets were empty of the basket women and costermongers, and swarming in lieu thereof with beggars and thieves; even the police, nipped at the heart by the frost, were harder on society that stopped the way, and had little mercy even on old faces. Mattie's was an old face which stopped the way at that time—Mattie, basketless and onionless, and trying lucifers again, and essaying on Saturday nights—when workmen's wages were paid—a song or two opposite the public-houses.

In this old fashion, Mattie earned a few pence at times; she was small for her age—very small—and the anxious-looking face touched those who had odd coppers to spare. But it was a task to live notwithstanding, and Mattie fought hard with the rest of the waifs and strays who had a tough battle to wage that winter time. "Luck went dead against her," as she termed it; she was barred from the market by want of capital—one lot of goods that she had speculated in never went off her hands, or rather her basket, on which they withered more and more with the frost, until they became unsaleable products—and there was no demand for lucifers or anything!

Mattie was nearly starving when the old tempter turned up in Great Suffolk Street—at the time when she was weak, and the police had been more than commonly "down on her," and she had not taken a halfpenny that day—at a time when the tempter *does* turn up as a general pile, that is, when we are waiting very anxiously for an EXCUSE.

"What! Mattie!—Lor! the sight o' time since I set eyes on you!"

"What! Mrs. Watts!"

"What are you doing, girl?—not much for yourself, I should think," with a disparaging glance at the tattered habiliments of our heroine.

"Not much just now, Mrs. Watts—hard lines it is."

"Ah! well, it may be—you allus wanted pluck, Mattie, like your mother. And hard lines it is just now, for those who stand nice about trifles. What's that in your hand, gal?"

"Congreve lights."

"What! still at Congreve lights—if I shouldn't hate the werry sight and smell on 'em by this time."

"So I do," said Mattie, sullenly.

"Come home with me, and let's have a bit o' talk together, Mattie—there's a friend or two o' your age a-coming to have a little talk with me to-night."

"Don't you keep a lodging house now?"

"No—a little shop for bones and bottles and such things; and we has a party in the back parler twice a week, and something nice and hot for supper."

"A school—on your own hook?" said Mattie, quickly.

"Oh! how sharp we gets as we grows up!—but you allus was as sharp as any needle, and I was only saying to Simes but yesterday, if I could just drop on little Mattie, she'd be the werry gal to do us credit—she would."

"I've been shifting for myself these last two years and odd, and I got on tidy till the frost set in, and now it's—*all up*!"

"Ah!—all up—precisely so."

Mrs. Watts did not detect the tragic element in Mattie's peroration; she had sallied forth in search of her, and had found her in the streets ragged and penniless and hungry. It was worth while to speculate in Mattie now—to show her some degree of kindness—to lure her back to the old haunts, and something worse than the old life. She began her temptations, and Mattie listened and trembled—the night was cold, and she had not tasted food that day. Mrs. Watts kept her hand upon the girl, and expatiated upon the advantages she had to offer now—even attempted to draw Mattie along with her.

"Wait a bit—don't be in a hurry," said Mattie; "I'll come presently p'raps—not just now."

"Oh! I'm not so sweet on you," said Mrs. Watts, aggrieved; "come if you like—stop away if you like—it's all one to me. I'll go about my rump-steaks for supper, and you can stay here and starve, if you prefer it."

This dialogue occurred only a short distance from Mr. Wesden's shop, when Mr. Wesden was putting up the shutters in his own quiet way, with very little noise, his boy having left him at a moment's notice. Mrs. Wesden, who had her fears for his back—Mr. W. had had a sensitive back for years—was dragging the shutters out from under the shop-board—thin slips of wood, that required not any degree of strength to manage. There were six shutters—at the third Mr. Wesden said—

"There's Mattie."

"Ah! poor girl!"

At the fifth he added—

"With an old woman that I don't like the style of very much."

Mrs. Wesden went to the door, and looked down the street at the tempter and the tempted—Mattie was under the lamp, and the face was a troubled one, on which the gas jet flickered. When the sixth shutter was up, and the iron band that secured them all firmly screwed into the door-post, the quiet couple stood side by side and watched the conflict to its abrupt conclusion. Both guessed what the subject had been—there was something of the night-bird and the gaol-bird about Mrs. Watts, that was easy of detection.

Mrs. Wesden touched her husband's arm.

"Danger, John."

"Ah!"

"And that girl has been a-going on so quietly for years, and getting her own living, and she without a father and a mother to care for her—not like our Harriet."

"No."

"And the way she brought back the money for that brooch."

"Yes—that was funny."

"I don't see the fun of it, John."

"That was good of her."

"Do you know, I've been thinking, John, we might find room for her—those boys are a great trouble to us, and if we had a girl, it might answer better to take the papers out, and she might serve in the shop."

"Serve in MY shop—good Lord!"

"Some day when we could trust her, I mean—and she could sleep with Ann; and I daresay she would come for her keep in these times. And we might be saving her—God knows from what!"

"Mrs. Wesden, you're as full of fancies as ever you can stick."

"I've a fancy to help her in these hard times, John; and when helping her won't ruin us—us who have put by now a matter of three thou——"

"Hush!"

"And when helping her won't ruin us, but get rid of those plagues of boys, John. Fancy our Harriet in the streets like that!"

She pointed to Mattie standing alone there, still under the gas lamp, deep in thought. Mr. Wesden looked, but his lined face was expressive of little sympathy, his wife thought.

"We're hard pushed for a boy—the bill's no sooner down than up again—try a girl, John!"

"If you'll get in out of the cold, Mrs. W., I'll think of it."

Mrs. Wesden retired, and Mr. Wesden kept his place by the open door, and his quiet eyes on Mattie. He was a man who did nothing in a hurry, and whose actions were ruled by grave deliberation. He did not confess to his wife that of late years he had been interested in Mattie; watched her from under his papers in the shop-window; saw her business-like habits, her method, her briskness over her scanty wares, her cleverness even in dodging her *bête noire* the policeman. He was a man, moreover, who went to church and read his Bible, and had many good thoughts beneath his occasional brusqueness and invariable immobility. A very quiet man, a man more than ordinarily cautious, hard to please, and still harder to rouse.

In shutting up his shop that night, he had caught one or two fragments of the dialogue, and he knew more certainly than his wife that Mattie was being tempted back to the old life. Of that life he knew everything; he had learned it piece by piece without affecting to take an interest in the matter; he even knew that Mattie had long taken a fancy—an odd fancy—to his daughter, that she often inquired about her, and her boarding-school, of Ann Packet, domestic to the house of Wesden.

He thought of Mattie's temptation, then of Mrs. Wesden's extraordinary suggestion. He was a lord of creation, and if he had a weakness it was in pooh-poohing the suggestions of his helpmate, although he adopted them in nine cases out of ten, disguising them, as he thought, by some little variation, and bringing them forward in due course as original productions of his own teeming brain.

And boys *had* worried him for years—lost his numbers, been behind-hand with the *Times* to his best customers, insulted those customers when reprimanded, and set the blame of delay at his door, played and fought with other boys before his very shop-front, broken his windows in putting up the shutters, had even paid visits to his till, and surreptitiously made off with stock, and had never in his memory of boys—industrious or otherwise—possessed one civil, clean-faced, decent youth.

"Suppose I had Mattie on trial for a week," he said at last, and looked towards the lamp-post. Mattie was gone—a black shadow, exactly like her, was hurrying away down the street towards the Borough—running almost, and with her hands to her head, as though a crowd of thoughts was stunning her!

Mr. Wesden never accounted for leaving his shop-door open without warning his wife—for running at his utmost speed after the girl.

At the corner of Great Suffolk Street he overtook her.

"Where are you going?—what are you running for?" he asked, indignantly.

Mattie started, looked at him, recognized him.

"Nothin—partic'ler—is anythink the matter?"

"How—how—should you—like—to be—*a news boy*?" he panted.

No circumlocution in Mr. Wesden—straight to the point as an arrow.

"Yours!—you wouldn't trust me—you never gives trust."

"I've—I've thought of trying you."

"You?" she said again.

"Yes—*me*."

"Well, I'd do anythink to get an honest living—but I was giving up the thoughts o' it—it's so hard for the likes of us, master."

"Come back, and I'll tell you what I've been thinking about, Mattie."

Not a word about what Mrs. Wesden had been thinking about—such is man's selfishness and narrow-mindedness.

Mattie went back—for good!

On this prologue to our story we can afford to drop the curtain, leaving our figures in outline, and waiting a better time to paint our characters—such as they are—more fully. We need not dwell upon Mattie's trial, upon Mattie's change of costume, and initiation into an old frock and boots of the absent Harriet—of the many accidents of life at Wesden, stationer's, accidents which led to the wanderer's settling down, a member of the household, an item in that household expenditure. Let the time roll on a year or two, during which Mr. Wesden's back grew worse, and Mrs. Wesden's hair more grey, and let the changes that have happened to our friends speak for themselves in the story we have set ourselves to write.

Leave we, then, the Stray on the threshold of her new estate, standing in Harriet Wesden's dress, thinking of her future; the shadow-land from which she has emerged behind her, and new scenes, new characters beyond there—beneath the bright sky, where all looks so radiant from the distance.

END OF THE FIRST BOOK.

BOOK II.

THE NEW ESTATE.

CHAPTER I.

HOME FOR GOOD.

Three years make but little difference in the general aspect of a poor neighbourhood. The same shops doing their scanty business; the same loiterers at street corners; the same watch from hungry eyes upon the loaves and fishes behind the window-glass; the same slip-shod men, women and children hustling one another on the pavement, in all weathers, "doing their bit of marketing;" the same dogs sniffing about the streets, and prowling round the butchers' shops.

An observer might detect many changes in the names over the shop fronts, certainly. Business goes wrong with a great many in three years—capital is small to work with in most instances, and when the rainy day comes, in due course, by the stern rule by which rainy days are governed, the resistance is feeble, and the weakest put the shutters up, sell off at an alarming sacrifice, and go, with wives and children, still further on the downhill road. There are seizures for rent, writs issued on delinquents, stern authority cutting off the gas and water, sterner authorities interfering with the weights and measures, which, in poor neighbourhoods, *will* get light occasionally; brokers' men making their quarterly raids, and still further perplexing those to whom life is a struggle, desperate and intense.

Amidst the changes in Great Suffolk Street, one business remains firm, and presents its wonted aspect. Over the little stationer's shop, the old established emporium for everything in a small way, is still inscribed the name of Wesden—has been repainted the name of Wesden in white letters, on a chocolate ground, as though there were nothing in the cares of business to daunt the tradesman who began life there, young and blooming!

There are changes amongst the papers in the windows—the sensation pennyworths—the pious pennyworths—the pennyworths started for the amelioration and mental improvement of the working classes, unfortunate pennyworths, that never get on, and which the working classes turn their backs upon, hating a moral in every other line as naturally as we do. The stock of volumes in the library is on the increase; the window, counter, shelves and drawers, are all well filled; Mr. Wesden deals in postage and receipt stamps—ever a good sign of capital to spare—and has turned the wash-house into a warehouse, where reams of paper, envelopes, and goods too numerous to mention, are biding their time to see daylight in Great Suffolk Street.

Changes are more apparent in the back-parlour, which has been home to Mr. and Mrs. Wesden for so many years. Let us look in upon them after three years' absence, and to the best of our ability note the alteration there.

Mr. and Mrs. Wesden are seated one on each side of the fire—Mr. Wesden in a new arm-chair, bought of an upholsterer in the Borough, an easy and capacious chair, with spring seats and sides, and altogether a luxury for that establishment. Mrs. Wesden has become very feeble and rickety; rheumatic fever—that last year's hard trial, in which she was given over, and the quiet man collapsed into a nervous child for the nonce—has left its traces, and robbed her of much energy and strength. She is a very old woman at sixty-three, grey-haired and sallow, with two eyes that look at you in an amiable, deer-like fashion—in a motherly way that gives you an idea of what a kind woman and good Christian she is.

Mr. Wesden, sitting opposite his worn better-half, was originally constructed from much tougher material. The lines are deeper in his face, the nose is larger, the eyes more sunken, perhaps the lips more thin, but there is business energy in him yet; no opportunity to earn money is let slip, and if it were not for constant twinges in his back, he would be as agile as in the old days when there were doubts of getting on in life.

But who is this sitting with them, like one of the family?—a dark-haired, pale-faced girl of sixteen, short of stature, neat of figure, certainly not pretty, decidedly not plain, with an everyday face, that might be passed fifty times, without attracting an observer; and then, on the fifty-first, startle him by its intense expression. A face older than its possessor's years; at times a grave face, more often, despite its pallor, a bright one—lit-up with the cheerful thoughts, which a mind at ease naturally gives to it.

Neatly, if humbly dressed—working with a rapidity and regularity that would have done credit to a stitching machine—evidently at home there in that back-parlour, to which her dark wistful eyes had been so often directed, in the old days; this is the Mattie of our prologue—the stray, diverted from the dark course it was taking, by the hand of John Wesden.

"Wesden, what's the time now?"

"My dear, it's not five minutes since you asked last," is the mild reproof of the husband, as he tugs at his copper-gilt watch chain for a while; "it's close on ten o'clock."

"I hope nothing has happened to the train—"

"What should happen, Mrs. Wesden?" says a brisk, clear ringing voice; "just to-night of all nights, when Miss Harriet is expected. Why, she didn't give us hope of seeing her till nine; and trains are always behind-hand, I've heard—and it's very early hours to get fidgety, isn't it, sir?"

"Much too early."

"I haven't seen my dear girl for twelve months," half moans the mother; "she'll come back quite a lady—she'll come back for good, Wesden, and be our pride and joy for ever. Never apart from us again."

"No, all to ourselves we shall have her after this. Well," with a strange half sigh, "we've done our duty by her, Mrs. W."

"I hope so."

"It's cost a heap of money—I don't regret a penny of it."

"Why should you, Wesden, when it's made our girl a lady—fit for any station in the world."

"But this perhaps," says Mr. Wesden, thoughtfully; "and this can't matter, now we——"

He does not finish the sentence, but takes his pipe down from the mantel-piece, and proceeds to fill it in a mechanical fashion. Mrs. Wesden looks at him quietly—her lord and husband never smokes before supper, without his mind is disturbed—the action reminds his wife that the supper hour is drawing near, and that nothing is prepared for Harriet's arrival.

"She will come home tired and hungry—oh! dear me—and nothing ready, perhaps."

"I'll help Ann directly," says Mattie.

The needle that has been plying all the time—that did not cease when Mattie attempted consolation—is stuck in the dress she is hemming; the work is rolled rapidly into a bundle; the light figure flits about the room, clears the table, darts down-stairs into the kitchen; presently appears with Ann Packet, maid-of-all-work, lays the cloth, sets knives and forks and plates; varies proceedings by attending to customers in the shop—Mattie's task more often, now Mr. Wesden's back has lost its flexibility—flits back again to the task of preparing supper in the parlour.

With her work less upon her mind, Mattie launches into small talk—her tongue rattles along with a rapidity only equal to her needle. She is in high spirits to-night, and talks more than usual, or else that loquacity for which a Mrs. Watts rebuked her once, has known no diminution with expanding years.

"We shall have her in a few more minutes, mistress," she says, addressing the feeble old woman in the chair; "just as if she'd never been away from us—

bless her pretty face!—and it was twelve days, rather than twelve months, since we all said good-bye to her. She left you on a sick bed, Mrs. Wesden, and she comes back to find you well and strong again—to find home just as it should be—everything going on well, and everybody—oh! so happy!"

"And to find you, Mattie—what?" asks Mr. Wesden, in his quiet way.

"To find me very happy, too—happy in having improved in my scholarship, such as it is, sir—happy with you two friends, to whom I owe—oh! more than I ever can think about, or be grateful enough for," she adds with an impetuosity that leads her to rush at the quiet man and kiss him on the forehead.

"We're square, Mattie—we're perfectly square now," he replies, settling his silver-rimmed spectacles more securely on his nose.

"Oh! that is very likely," is the sharp response.

"You nursed the old lady like a daughter—you saved her somehow. If it hadn't been for you——"

"She would have been well weeks before, only I was such a restless girl, and wouldn't let her be quiet," laughs Mattie.

She passes into the shop again with the same elastic tread, serves out two ounces of tobacco, detects a bad shilling, and focuses the customer with her dark eyes, appears but little impressed by his apologies, and more interested in her change, locks the till, and is once more in the parlour, talking about Miss Harriet again.

"She is on her way now," she remarks; "at London Bridge by this time, and Master Hinchford—we must say Mr. Hinchford now, I suppose—helping her into the cab he's been kind enough to get for her."

"What's the time now, Wesden?" asks the mother.

"Well," after the usual efforts to disinter—or disembowel—the silver watch, "it's certainly just ten."

"And by the time Tom's put the shutters up, she'll be here!" cries Mattie; "see if my words don't come true, Mr. Wesden."

"Well, I hope they will; if they don't, I—I think I'll just put on my hat, and walk down to the station."

Presently somebody coming down-stairs with a heavy, regular tread, pausing at the side door in the parlour, and giving two decisive raps with his knuckles on the panels.

"Come in."

Enter Mr. Hinchford, senior, with his white hair rubbed the wrong way, and his florid face looking somewhat anxious.

"Haven't they come yet?"

"Not yet, sir."

"Ah! I suppose not," catching Mattie's glance directed towards him across the needlework which she has resumed again, and at which she is working harder than ever; "there's boxes to find, and pack on the cab, and Miss Harriet's no woman if she do not remember at the last minute something left behind in the carriage."

"Won't you sit down, sir?" asks Mrs. Wesden.

"N—no, thank you," he replies; "you'll have your girl home in a minute, and we mustn't over-crowd the little parlour. I shall give up my old habit of smoking here, now the daughter comes back—you must step up into my quarters, Wesden, a little more often."

"Thank you."

"Temporary quarters, I suppose, we must say, now the boy's getting on so well. Thank God," with a burst of affection, "that I shall see that boy in a good position of life before I die."

"He's a clever lad."

"Clever, sir!" ejaculates the father, "he's more than clever, though I don't sing his praises before his face. He has as clear a head-piece as any man of forty, and he's as good a man of business."

"And so steady," adds Mrs. Wesden.

"God bless you! madam, yes."

"And so saving," is the further addition of Mr. Wesden,—"that's a good sign."

"Ah! he knows the value of money better than his father did at his age," says the old man; "with his caution, energy, and cleverness we shall see him, if we live, a great man. Whoever lives to see him—a great man!"

"It's a comfort when our children grow up blessings to us," remarks Mrs. Wesden, dreamily looking at the fire; "neither you nor I, sir, have any cause to be sorry for those we love so very, very much."

"No, certainly not. We're lucky people in our latter days—good night."

"You can't stop, then?" asked Wesden.

"Not just now. Don't keep the boy down here, please—he'll stand and talk, forgetting that he's in the way to-night, unless you give him a hint to the contrary. Out of business, he's a trifle inconsiderate, unless you plainly tell him he's not wanted. Good night—I shall see Harriet in the morning."

"Yes—good night."

Mr. Hinchford retires again, and in a few minutes afterwards, before there is further time to dilate upon the danger of railway travelling, and the uncertainty of human hopes, the long-expected cab dashes up to the door. There is a bustle in Great Suffolk Street; the cabman brings in the boxes amidst a little knot of loungers, who have evidently never seen a box before, or a cab, or a young lady emerge therefrom assisted by a tall young man, or listened to an animated dispute about a cab-fare, which comes in by way of sequence whilst the young lady is kissing everybody in turn in the parlour.

"My fare's eighteenpence, guv'nor."

"Not one shilling, legally," affirmed the young man.

"I never did it for a shilling afore—I ain't a going now—I'll take a summons out first."

"Take it."

"You won't stand another sixpence, guv'nor?"

"No."

"Then," bundling on to his box, and lashing his horse ferociously, "I won't waste my time on a tailor—it's much too valuable for that!"

The young man laughs at this withering sarcasm, and passes through the shop into the parlour, where the animation has scarcely found time to subside.

Harriet Wesden is holding Mattie at arm's length, and looking steadily at her—the stationer's daughter is taller by a head than the stray.

"And you, Mattie, have been improving, I see—learning all the lessons that I set you before I went away—becoming of help to father and mother, and thinking of poor *me* sometimes."

"Ah! very often of 'poor me.'"

"Oh! how tired I am!—how glad I shall be to find myself in my room! Now, Mr. Sidney, I'm going to bid you good night at once, thanking you for all past services."

"Very well, Miss Harriet."

"And, goodness me!—I did not notice those things before! What! spectacles, Sidney—at your age?"

The tall young man colours and laughs—keeping his position at the door-post all the while.

"Can't afford to have weak eyes yet, and so have sacrificed all my personal charms for the sake of convenience in matters of business. You don't mean to say that they look so very bad, though?"

"You look nearer ninety than nineteen," she replies. "Oh! I wouldn't take to spectacles for ever so much."

"That's a very different affair," remarks Sidney.

"Why?"

"Oh! because it *is*—that's all. Well, I think I'll say good night now—shall I take that box up-stairs for you, Miss Harriet?"

"Ann and I can manage it, Mr. Hinchford," says Mattie.

"Yes, and put a rib out, or something. Can't allow the gentler sex to be black slaves during my sojourn in Great Suffolk Street. Good night all."

"Good night."

He closes the shop door, seizes the box which has been deposited in the shop, swings it round on his shoulders, and marches up-stairs with it two steps at a time, and whistling the while. On the landing, outside the sitting-room, and double-bedded room, which his father occupies, Ann Packet, domestic servant, meets him with a light.

"Lor a mussy on us!—is that you, Master Sidney?"

"Go a-head, up-stairs, wench, and let us find a place to put the box down. This is Miss Harriet's box."

"Orful heavy, ain't it, sir?"

"Well—it's not so light as it might be," asserts Master Sidney; "forward, there."

Meanwhile, too tired to repair to her room for any toilette arrangements at that hour of the night, Harriet Wesden sits down between her mother and father, holding her bonnet on her lap. Mr. and Mrs. Wesden regard her proudly, as well they may, Harriet being a girl to be proud of—tall, graceful, and pretty, something that makes home bright to the parents, and has been long missed by them. No one is aware of all that they have sacrificed in their desire to make a lady of their only child—or of one-half of the hopes which they have built upon concerning her.

"This always seems such an odd, *little* box to come back to after the great Brighton school," she says, wearily; "oh, dear! how tired I am!"

"Get your supper, my dear, at once, and don't sit up for anybody to-night," suggests the mother.

"I don't want any supper. I—I think I'll go up-stairs at once and keep all my little anecdotes of school and schooling till the morrow. Shall I?"

"By all means, Harriet, if you're tired," says the father, "but after a long journey I would take something. You don't feel poorly, my dear?"

"Who?—I—oh! no," she answered, startled at the suggestion; "but I have been eating biscuits and other messes all the journey up to London, and therefore my appetite is spoiled for the night. To-morrow I shall be myself again—and we will have a long talk about all that has happened since I left here last year—by to-morrow, we shall have settled down so comfortably!"

"I hope so."

She looks timidly towards her father, but he is smoking his pipe, and placidly surveying her. She kisses him, then her mother, lastly Mattie, and leaves the room;—the instant afterwards Mattie remembers the unwieldy box, which Master, or Mr. Hinchford has carried up-stairs.

"She'll never uncord the box—I should like to help her, if you can spare me."

"Knots always did try the dear girl," affirms Mrs. Wesden, "go and help her by all means—my dear."

Mattie needs no second bidding; she darts from the room, and in a few minutes is at the top of the house; in her forgetfulness inside the room without so much as a "By your leave, Miss Wesden."

"Oh! dear, I forgot to knock—and oh! dear, dear!" rushing forward to Harriet sitting by the bedside and rocking herself to and fro, as though in pain, "what is the matter?—can I help you?—what has happened!"

CHAPTER II.

A GIRL'S ROMANCE.

Miss Wesden continued to rock herself to and fro and moan at frequent intervals, after Mattie had intruded so unceremoniously upon her sorrows. She had reached the hysterical stage, and there was no stopping the tears and the little windy sobs by which they were varied—and Harriet Wesden in tears, the girl whom Mattie had reverenced so long, was too much for our small heroine.

"Oh! dear—what has happened?—shall I run and tell your father and mother?"

"Oh! for goodness sake, don't think of anything of the kind!" cried the startled Harriet; "I—I—I shall be better in a minute. It's only a spasm or something—it's nothing that any one—can—help me—with!"

"I know what it is," remarked Mattie, after a moment's reflection.

"You—*you* do, Mattie!"

"It's the wind," was the matter-of-fact reply; "you've been eating a heap of nasty buns, and then come up here without your supper—and it's brought on spasms, as you say."

"How ridiculous you are, child!" said this woman of seventeen, parting her fair hair back from her face, and making an effort to subdue her agitation; "don't you see that I am very, very miserable!"

"In earnest?"

"Are people ever really, truly miserable in fun, Mattie?" was the sharp rejoinder.

"Not truly miserable, I should fancy. But you—oh! Miss Harriet, you miserable, at your age!"

"Yes—it's a fact."

"Perhaps you have been robbed," suggested the curious Mattie; "I know that they used to send them out from Kent Street to hang about the railway stations. Never mind, Miss Harriet, I have been earning money, lately; and if you don't want your father to know how careless you have been——"

"Always unselfish—always thinking of doing some absurd action, that shall benefit any one of the name of Wesden. No, no, Mattie, it's not money, it's not that—that vulgar complaint you mentioned just now. Oh! to have one friend in the world in whom I could trust—in whom I could confide my misery!"

"And haven't you *one*?" was the soft answer.

Harriet looked up at the wistful face—so full of love and pity.

"Ah! there's *you*—you mean. But you are a child still, and would never understand me. *You* would never have sympathy with all that I have suffered, or keep my secret if you had."

"What I could understand, I cannot say—I'm still hard at work, in over-time, at my lessons—but you may be sure of my sympathy, and of my silence. It's not that I'm so curious, Miss Harriet—but that I hope, when I know all, to be a comfort to you."

Harriet shook her head despondently, and beat her tiny foot impatiently upon the carpet. Any one in the world to be a comfort to her, was a foolish idea, that only irritated her to allude to.

"I'm living here to be a comfort to you all," said Mattie, in a low voice; "I've set myself to be that, if ever I can. Every one in this house helped in a way to take me from the streets; every one has been more kind to me than I deserved—helped me on—given me good advice—done so much for me! I—I have often thought that perhaps my time might come some day to your family, or the Hinchfords; but if to you, my darling, whom I love before the whole of them—who has been more than kind—whom I loved when I was a little ragged girl in the dark streets outside—how happy I shall be!"

"Happy to see me miserable, Mattie—that's what *that* amounts to."

"I didn't mean that," answered Mattie, half-aggrieved.

"No, I'm sure you did not," was the reply. "Lock the door, my dear, and let me take you into my confidence—I *do* want some one to talk to about it terribly!"

Mattie locked the door, and, full of wonder, sat down by Harriet Wesden's side. The stationer's daughter had always treated Mattie as a companion rather than as a servant; she had but seen her in her holidays of late years—her father had trusted Mattie and made a shop-woman of her—she had found Mattie constituted after a while one of the family—Mattie was only a year her junior, and Mattie's love, almost her idolatry for her, had won upon a nature which, though far from faultless, was at least susceptible to kindness, ever touched by affection, and ever ready to return both.

"You must know, Mattie, then—and pray never breathe a syllable of this to mortal soul again—that I'm in love."

"*Lor!*" gasped Mattie.

"Dreadfully and desperately in love."

"Oh! hasn't it come early—and oh! *ain't* I dreadfully sorry."

"Hush, Mattie, not so loud. They'll be coming up to bed in the next room presently, and if they were to find it out, I should die."

"They wouldn't mind, after they had once got used to it," said Mattie; "and if it has really come to love in earnest—there's a good deal of sham love I've been told—why, I don't think there's anything to cry about. I should dance for joy myself."

"You're too young to know what you're talking about, Mattie," reproved Harriet.

"No, I'm not," was the quick answer; "I should feel very happy to know that there was some one to love me better than anybody in the world—to think of me first—pray about me before he went to bed at night—dream of me till the daytime—keep me always in his head. Why, shouldn't I be happy to know this, I who never remember what love was from anybody?"

"Yes, yes, I understand you, Mattie," said Harriet; "that's part of love—not all."

"What else is there?"

Mattie was evidently extremely curious concerning all phases of "the heart complaint."

"It's too complicated, Mattie; when you're a woman, you'll be able to find out for yourself. It's better not to trouble your head about it yet awhile."

"I wish you hadn't, Miss Harriet. It's not the likes of me that is going to think about it; and if you had left it till you were really a woman—I don't know much about the matter yet—but I'm thinking it would be all the better for you, too, my dear."

"It came all of a rush like—I wasn't thinking of it. There were two young men at first, who used to watch our school, and laugh at the biggest of us, and kiss their hands—just as young men *will* do, Mattie."

"Like their impudence, I think."

Mattie's matter-of-fact views were coming uppermost again. She had seen much of the world in her youth, experienced much hardship, worked hard for a living, and there was no romance in her disposition—only affection, which had developed of late years, thanks to her new training.

"But there's always a little fun amongst the big girls, Mattie."

"What is the governess about?"

"She's looking out—but, bless you, she may look!"

"Ah! I suppose so. Well?"

"And then one young man went away, and only one was left—the handsomer of the two—and he fell in love *with me*!"

"Really and truly?"

"Why, of course he did. Is it so wonderful?" and the boarding-school girl looked steadily at her companion.

Mattie looked at her. She *was* a beautiful girl, and perhaps it was not so wonderful, after all. But then Mattie still looked at Harriet Wesden as a child—even as a child younger than she whom the world had aged very early—rendered "old-fashioned," as the phrase runs, in many things.

"Not wonderful, perhaps—but wasn't it wrong?" asked Mattie.

"I don't think so—I never thought of that—he was very fond of me, and used to send me letters by the servant, and I—I did get very fond of him. He was a gentleman's son, and oh! *so* handsome, Mattie, and *so* tall, and *so* clever!"

"About your age, I suppose?"

"No, four-and-twenty, or more, perhaps. I don't know."

"Well?—oh! dear, how *did* it end?" asked Mattie; "it's like the story-books in the shop—isn't it?"

"Wait awhile, dear. The misery of the human heart is to be unfolded now. He's a gentleman's son, and there's an estate or something in West India or East India, or in some dreadful hot place over the water somewhere, where the natives hook themselves in the small of their backs, and swing about and say their prayers."

"How nasty!"

"And—and he—was to go there," her sobs beginning again at the reminiscence, "and live there, and," dropping her voice to a whisper, "he asked me if I'd run away with him, and be married to him over there."

Mattie clenched her fist spasmodically. She saw through the flimsy veil of romance, with a suddenness for which she was unprepared herself. She was a woman of the world, with a knowledge of the evil in it, on the instant.

"Oh! that man was a big scamp, I'm sure of it—I know it!"

"What makes you think that?" asked Harriet, imperiously.

"Couldn't he have come to Suffolk Street, and told your father all about it like a—like a man?"

"Yes, but *his* father—his father is a gentleman, and would never let him marry a poor, deplorable stationer's daughter."

"Ah! his father does not know you, and his father didn't have the chance of trying, I'm inclined to think," was the shrewd comment here.

"Never mind that," said Harriet, "I don't see that that's anything to do with the matter just now. I wouldn't run away; I was very frightened; I loved father and mother, and I knew how they loved me. And when I cried, he said he had only done it to try me, and then—and then—he went away next day for ever!"

"And a good riddance," muttered Mattie.

"Oh! Mattie, you cruel, *cruel* girl, is this the sympathy you talked about a little while ago?"

"I've every sympathy with you, my own dear young lady," said Mattie; "I'm sorry to see how this is troubling you—you so young!—just now. But I don't think *he* acted very properly, Miss Harriet, or that you were quite so careful of yourself as—as you might have been."

"I'm a wretched, wretched woman!"

"Does he know where you live?"

"Ye—es," she sobbed.

"And where did he live before he went to India?"

"Surrey."

"That's a large place, I think. I haven't turned to geography lately, but I fancy it's a double map. If that's all the address, it's a good big one. May I ask his name?"

"Never," was the melodramatic answer.

"Ah! it does not matter much. I hope, for the sake of all down-stairs, you will try and forget it. It's no credit; you were much too young, and he too old in everything. Oh! Miss Harriet, you and the other young ladies must have been going it down at Brighton!"

"It all happened suddenly, Mattie; I'm not a forward girl; they're all of my age—oh! and ever so much bolder."

"A very nice school that must be, I should think," said Mattie, leaving the bed for the box, which she proceeded to uncord; "if I ever hear of anybody wanting to send their daughters to a finishing akkademy," Mattie was not thoroughly up in pure English yet, "I'll just recommend that one!"

"Mattie," reproved Harriet, "you've got at all that you wanted to know, and now you're full of bitter sarcasm."

"I'm full of bitter nothing, Miss," was the reply; "and oh!—you don't know how sorry I feel that it has all happened, making you so old and womanly, before your time—filling your head with rubbish about—the chaps!"

Harriet said nothing—she sat and watched with dreamy eyes the process of uncording; only, when Mattie attempted to turn the box on its side, did she spring up and help to assist without a word.

"There, that'll do," she said peevishly; "let me only unlock the box, and get at my night-things, that's all I want. Mattie, for goodness sake, don't keep so in the way!"

Mattie stood aside, and Harriet Wesden, with an impatient hand, unlocked the box, and raised the heavy oaken lid. Mattie's eyes, sharp as needles, detected a small roll of written papers, neatly tied.

"Are these the letters, Miss Harriet?"

"Good gracious me, how curious and prying you are!" said Harriet, snatching the packet from her hand. "I wish I had never told you a syllable—I wish you'd leave my things alone!"

"I beg your pardon—I only asked. It *was* wrong."

"Well, there, I forgive you; but you are so tiresome, and old-fashioned. I can't make you out—I never shall—you're not like other girls."

"Was I brought up like other girls, you know?" was the sad question.

"No, no—I forgot that—I beg your pardon, Mattie; I didn't mean it for a taunt."

"God bless you, I know that. What are you doing?"

"Getting rid of these," thrusting the letters in the candle flame as she spoke. "I can trust you, but not them, Mattie."

"I'd hold them over the fire-place, then. If they drop on the toilet-table, we shall have the house a-fire."

Harriet took the advice proffered, and removed her combustibles to the place recommended. Mattie, on her knees by the box, watched the process.

"And there's an end of *them*," Harriet said at last, in a decisive tone.

"And of him—say of him?"

"We parted for ever—but I shall always think of him—think, too, that perhaps I *was* very young and thoughtless and vain, to lead him on, or to be led on. But oh! Mattie, he did love me—he wouldn't have harmed me for the world!"

"He hasn't spoken of writing—you haven't promised to write any more."

"No—it was a parting for *ever*. Haven't I said so, over and over again?"

"Then you'll soon forget him, Miss Harriet—try and forget him, for your own sake—you can't tell whether he wasn't making game of you, for certain; he didn't act well, for he wasn't a boy, was he? And now go to sleep, and wake up in the morning your old self, Miss."

"I'll try—I must try!"

"I don't think that this fine gentleman will ever turn up again; if he does, you'll be older to take your own part. Oh! dear, how contrary things do go, to be sure."

"What's the matter now?"

"I did think I knew whom you were to marry."

"Who was it?" said Harriet, with evident interest in her question.

"Well, I thought, Miss Harriet, that you'd grow up, and grow up to be a young woman, and that Master Sidney underneath, would grow up, and grow up to be a young man, and you'd fall naturally in love with one another—marry, and be oh! so happy. When I'm hard at work at the lessons he or his father writes out for me sometimes, I catch myself forgetting all about them, and thinking of you and him together—and I your servant, perhaps, or little housekeeper. I've always thought that that would come to pass some day, and that he'd grow rich, and make a lady of you—and it made me happy to think that the two, who'd been perhaps the kindest in all the world to me, would marry some fine day. I've pictered it—pictured it," she corrected, "many and many a time, until I fancied at last it must come true."

"Master Sidney, indeed!" was the disparaging comment.

"When you know him, you won't talk like that," said Mattie; "he's a gentleman—growing like one fast—and I don't think, young as he is, that he would have acted like that other one you've been silly enough to think about."

"Silly!—oh! Mattie, Mattie, that isn't sympathy with me—I don't know whether you're a child, or an old woman—you talk like both of them, and in one breath. Why did I tell you!—why did I tell you!"

"Because I was in earnest, and begged hard—because I was afraid, and you could not keep such a secret from me as that; and if you had wanted help—how I would have stood by you!"

Harriet noted the kindling eyes, and her heart warmed to the nondescript.

"Thank you, Mattie—one friend at least now."

"Always,—don't you think so?"

"Yes, I do."

Mattie was at the door, when Harriet called her back.

"Mattie, never a word about this again. I daresay I shall soon forget it, for I am very young; and though it was LOVE, yet I won't let it break my heart. I'm very wretched now. I shall be glad," she added with a yawn, "to lie down and think of all my sorrows."

"And sleep them away."

"Oh! I shall not close an eye to-night. Good night, Mattie."

Miss Harriet Wesden, a young lady who had begun life early, was sleeping soundly three minutes after Mattie's departure from the room.

CHAPTER III.

OUR CHARACTERS.

In our last chapter we have implied that life began early for Harriet Wesden. Before her school-days were finished, and with that precocity for which school-girls of the present era are unhappily distinguished, she was thinking of her lover, and constituting herself the heroine of a little romance, all the more dangerous for being unreal and out of the common track. A tender-hearted girl, with a head not the most strong in the world, is easily impressed by the sentiment, real or assumed, of the first good-looking young fellow whom she may meet. In her own opinion she is not too young to receive admiration, and the consciousness of having impressed one of the opposite sex, arouses her vanity, changes the current of her thoughts, makes the world for awhile a very different place—bright, etherial and unreal. All this very dangerous ground to tread, but the more delightful for its pitfalls; all this a something that has occurred in a greater or less degree to most of us in our time, though we have the good sense to say nothing about it, or to laugh at the follies and the troubles we rashly sought in our nonage. Boys and girls begin their courtships early in these latter days—there is not a girl of sixteen who does not consider herself fit to love and be loved, however demure she may appear, or however much she may be kept back by detestable short frocks and frilled indescribables. And as for our boys, why, they are men of the world immediately they leave school—men of a world that is growing more rapid in its revolutions, and hardens its inhabitants wonderfully fast. It is a singular fact in the history of shop-keeping, that children's toys are becoming unfashionable. "Bless you, sir, children don't buy toys now, they're much too old for those amusements!" was the assertion of one of the trade to the writer of this work. And how many little misses and masters can most of us call to mind who are growing pale over their fancy work, their books, and their "collections," children who will do anything but play, and have souls above "Noah's Arks."

Therefore, in these precocious times, Harriet Wesden, seventeen next month, was no exceptional creature; moreover, she had been to a boarding-school, where she had met with many of her own age who were twice as womanly and worldly—big girls, who were always talking about "the chaps," as Mattie had inelegantly phrased it.

There is no occasion in this place to retrace the school-career of Harriet Wesden, to see how much she has kept back or extenuated; her story to Mattie was a truthful one, told with no drawbacks, but with a half-pride in her achievements which her girlish sorrows were not capable of concealing. There was something satisfactory in having loved and having been loved; and though the love had vanished away, still the reminiscence was not wholly painful, however much she might fancy so at that period.

Mattie had listened to her story, and offered all the consolation in her power; Mattie was a girl of hard, plain facts, and looked more soberly at the world than her contemporaries. She had a dark knowledge of the worst part of it, and her early years had aged her more than she was aware of herself—aged her thoughts rather than her heart, for she was always cheerful, and her spirits were never depressed; she went her way in life quietly and earnestly, grateful for the great change by which that life had been characterized; grateful to all who had helped to turn it in a different channel. At this period, Mattie was happy; there was nothing to trouble her; it was an important post to hold in that stationer's shop; everybody had confidence in her, and had given her kind words; she had learned to know right from wrong; they were interested in her moral progress, both the shopkeeper and the lodgers on the first floor; she was more than content with her position in society—she was thankful for it.

The Hinchfords had maintained their interest in Mattie, from the day of her attempt to explain her long search for the brooch. The father, a student of human nature, as he termed himself, had persuaded her to attend evening school, to study to improve in reading and writing at home; and Master Hinchford, who wrote a capital hand, set her copies in his leisure, and gave his verdict on her calligraphic performances. Mattie snatched at the elements of her education in a fugitive manner; Mr. Wesden did not object to her progress, but she was his servant, afterwards his shop-woman, and he wanted his money's worth out of her, like a man who understood business in all its branches. Mattie never neglected work for her studies, and yet made rapid advancement; and, by-and-bye, Mr. Hinchford, during one of his quiet interviews with the stationer, had obtained for her more time to attend her evening classes—and hence the improvement which we have seen in Mattie. So time had gone on, till Miss Wesden's return for good—so far, then, had the stationer's daughter and the stray made progress.

Mattie, with a judgment beyond her years, had perceived the evanescent nature of Harriet Wesden's romance, and prophesied concerning it. She did not believe in the depth or intensity of Harriet's sorrow; moreover, she knew Harriet was not of a fretful disposition, and that new faces and new pursuits would exercise their usual effect upon a nature impressionable, and—just a little weak! Mattie was a judge of character without being aware of it, and her own unimpressionability set her above her fellows, and gave her a clear insight into events that were passing around her. A girl of observation also, who let few things—serious or trivial—escape her, but glanced at them in their revolutions, and remembered them, if necessary. This acuteness had possibly been derived from her hand-to-mouth existence in the old days; in her time of affluence, the habit of storing up and taking mental notes of everything, had not deserted her. Take her altogether, she was a sharp girl, and suited Mr. Wesden's business admirably.

Quietly Mattie set herself to take stock of Harriet Wesden, after the latter's confession, to note if the love to which she had confessed were likely to be a permanency or not. Harriet and Mattie spoke but little concerning the adventures at Brighton; Mattie shunned the subject, and turned the conversation when Harriet felt prone to dilate upon her melancholy sensations. Besides, Mattie knew her place, kept to the shop, whither Harriet seldom followed her—that young lady having a soul above the business, by which she had benefited. Mr. and Mrs. Wesden rather admired this; they had saved money, and the business, to the latter at least, was but a secondary consideration; they had paid a large sum to make a lady of Harriet, and when they retired from business, Harriet would go with them, and be their hope and comfort, with her lady-like ways, in their little suburban residence. They were not slow in letting Harriet know this; they spoke of a private life very frequently; when Harriet was two years older, they would retire and live happily ever afterwards! Or, Mr. Wesden thought more prudently, if they did not give up the business for good, still they would live away from it, and leave the management of it to some trustworthy personage—Mattie, for instance, who would see after their interests, whilst they took their ease in their old age.

Mr. Hinchford, senior, had listened to these flying remarks more than once; he spoke of his own establishment in the future in *his* turn—where and how he should live with that clever boy of his, who would redeem the family credit by assuming the Hinchfords' legitimate position.

"I kept my carriage once, Mr. Wesden—I hope to do it again. My boy's very clever, very energetic—he has gained the esteem of his employers, and I believe that they will make a partner of him some day."

What Sidney Hinchford believed, did not appear upon the surface. He was a youth—say a young man—who kept a great many thoughts to himself, and pushed on in life steadily and undemonstratively. His father was right; Sidney had gained the esteem of his employers; he *was* very clever at figures, handy as a correspondent, never objected to over-work, did more work than any one of the old hands; evinced an aptitude for business and an interest in his employers' success—very remarkable in these egotistical times. His employers were wholesale tea-dealers in Mincing Lane—well-to-do men, without families of their own—men who had risen from the ranks, after the fashion of City-men, who have a nice habit of getting on in the world. Sidney Hinchford's manner pleased them, but they kept their own counsel, and watched his progress—and Sidney's was a remarkable progress, for a youth of his age.

Sidney, be it said here, was an ambitious youth in his heart. His father had been a rich man; his father's family, from which they held themselves aloof, were rich people, and his hope was in recovering the ground which, by some means or other never satisfactorily explained to him, the Suffolk Street lodgers had managed to lose. Young men brought up in City counting-houses have a wonderful reverence for money; Sidney saw its value early in life, and became just a trifle too careful; for over-carefulness makes a man suspicious, and keeps the heart from properly expanding with love and charity to those who need it. An earnest and an honourable young man, as we hope to prove without labelling our character at the outset, yet he stood too much upon what was legal, what was a fair price, or a good bargain, and pushed his way onwards without much thought for the condition of beings less lucky than he. There was a prize ahead of him; he could see it above the crowd which jostled him for bread, for fame, for other prizes worth the winning, and by which he set no store, and he kept his eyes upon it steadfastly and dreamed of it in his sleep. He became grave-faced and stern before his time—he was a man at nineteen, with a man's thoughts, and doing a man's work.

And then a something came to soften him and turn his thoughts a little aside from the beaten track, and this is how it came about.

CHAPTER IV.

A NEW ADMIRER.

Master Sidney Hinchford in old times had been a playfellow of Harriet Wesden—lodging in the same house together, returning from school at the same hours, they had become almost brother and sister, entertaining for each other that child's affection, which it was but natural to expect would have been developed under the circumstances.

Mr. Hinchford, a widower, with no great ability in the management of children, was glad to see his boy find an attraction in the stationer's parlour, and leave him to the study of his books or the perusal of his newspapers, after the long office-hours. He was a thoughtful man, too, who considered it best for his son to form a friendship with one of his own age; and he had become attached to the Wesdens, as people who had been kind to him and his boy in a great trouble. And it was satisfactory to pair off Harriet Wesden—who was in the way of business, and generally considered at that period a tiresome child, seldom of one mind longer than five minutes together—with Master Hinchford, and so keep her out of mischief and out of the shop where the draughts were many and likely to affect her health. This good understanding had never diminished between Harriet Wesden and Sidney Hinchford; only the boarding-school at last had set them apart. When they met once a year, they were still the same warm friends, and it was like a brother meeting a sister when the Christmas holidays came round. The last holiday but one, when Harriet, who had grown rapidly, returned from Brighton, a girl close upon sixteen years of age, there was a little shyness at first between them, which wore off in a few days. Sidney met her after a year's absence without kissing her, stared and stammered, and found it hard to assume a natural demeanour, and it was only Harriet's frank and girlish ways that eventually set him at his ease.

The present Christmas all was altered, very much for the worse, Sidney thought. He had met, for the first time, a pale-faced, languishing young lady—a lady who had become very beautiful certainly, but was not the Harriet Wesden whom he had hitherto known. He had escorted her from the Brighton station, thinking that she had altered very much, and that he did not like her new ways half so well as the old; he had seen her every evening after that return, noted the variableness of her moods, set her down, in his critical way, for an eccentric girl, whom it was impossible to understand.

If she were dull, he fancied he had offended her; if she were lively, he became thin-skinned enough to imagine that she was making fun of him. He did not like it, he thought; but he found the new Harriet intruding upon his business ideas, getting between him and the rows of figures in his ledger, perplexing him with the last look she gave him, and the last musical word that had rung in his ears. He did not believe that he was going to fall in love with her—not when he was really in love with her, and found his sensations a nuisance.

And Harriet Wesden, who had already succumbed to the love-god, and been enraptured by the dulcet notes of the stranger, she thought Sidney Hinchford had not improved for the better; that his glasses rendered him almost plain, that his dry hard voice grated on her ears, and that he had even grown quite a cross-looking young man. She took occasion to tell him these unpleasant impressions with a sisterly frankness to which he appeared to object; gave him advice as to deportment, set of his neckerchief, size of his gloves, and only became a little thoughtful when she noted the effect which her advice had upon him, and the lamb-like docility with which he obeyed all her directions. Finally, all her spirits came back; she had her doubts as to the state of Sidney Hinchford's heart, and whether her first judgment on his personal appearance were correct in the main; she began to observe him more closely; life appeared to present an object in it once more; her vanity—for she was a girl who knew she was pretty, and was proud of the influence which her pretty face exercised—was flattered by his rapt attention; and though she should never love anybody again—never, never in all her life!—yet it was pleasant to know that Sidney was thinking of her, and to see how a smile or a frown of hers brightened his looks or cast them back into shadow.

Harriet Wesden was partial to experimentalizing on the effect which her appearance might create on society. She was not a strong-minded girl, who despised appearances; on the contrary, as weak and as vain as that Miss Smith or Miss Brown, whose demerits our wives discuss over their tea-tables. She was not strong-minded—she was pretty—and she was seventeen years of age!

If she went for a walk, or on a shopping excursion, she was particular about the bonnet she wore; and if young men, and old men too, some of them, looked admiringly at her pretty face as they passed her, she was flattered at the attention in her heart, although she kept steadily on her way, and looked not right or left in her progress. If the army of nondescripts in the great drapers' was thrown into a small flutter at her appearance therein, and white neckclothed servility struggled behind the boxes for the distinction of waiting on her, it was a gratification which she felt all the more for remaining so lady-like and unmoved on the high chair before the counter. She was a girl who knew her attractions, and was proud of them; but unfortunately she was a girl who knew but little else, and who thought but of little else just then. There was a pleasure in knowing that, let her step into any part of the London streets, people would notice her, even stop and look after her; and it did not strike her that there were other faces as pretty as hers, who received the same amount of staring and gaping at, and met with the same little "romantic" incidents occasionally.

From her boarding-school days, Harriet had been inclined to romance; the one foolish *escapade* had tinged life with romantic hues, and pretty as she was, her opinion of her own good looks was considerably higher than any one else's. She passed through life from seventeen to eighteen years of age taking everything as a compliment—flattered by the rude stares, the impertinent smiles from shallow-brained puppies who leer at every woman *en route*; rather pleased than otherwise if a greater idiot or a nastier beast than his contemporaries tracked her footsteps homewards, and lingered about Great Suffolk Street in the hope of seeing her again. All this the spell of her beauty which lured men towards her; all this without one thought of harm—simply an irresistible vanity that took delight in her influence, and was pleased with immoderate fooleries.

Pretty, vain, foolish, and fond of attention, on the one side; but good-tempered, good-hearted, and innocent of design on the other. A butterfly disposition, that would carry its owner through life if the sun shone, but would be whirled heaven knows where in a storm. She would have been happy all her life, had all mankind been up to the dead level of honest intentions, which it is not, just at present, thanks to the poor wretches like us who get our living by story-telling.

Most young ladies constituted like Harriet Wesden have an ordeal to pass through for better for worse; if for worse, God help them! Harriet Wesden's came in due course.

It was, in the beginning, but another chapter of romance—another conquest! Love at first sight in London Streets, and the fervour of a new-born passion carrying the devotee out of the track, and leading him to follow in her footsteps, worshipping at a distance. It had occurred twice before, and was a compliment to the power of her charms—her heart quite fluttered at these little breaks in a somewhat monotonous existence. It was rather aggravating that the romance always ended in an old-fashioned bookseller's shop in Great Suffolk Street, where "the mysterious strangers" were jostled into the mud by people with baskets, and then run down by bawling costers with barrows. That was not a nice end to the story, and though she wished the story to conclude at the door, yet she would have preferred something more graceful as a "wind-up." Nevertheless, take it for all in all, a satisfactory proof that she had a face pretty enough to lure people out of their way, and rob them of their time—lead them without a "mite of encouragement" on her part to follow her fairy footsteps. If there were hypocrisy in her complaints to Mattie concerning the "impudence" of the fellows, she scarcely knew it herself; and Mattie would not believe in hypocrisy in the girl whom she served with a

Balderstonian fidelity. The third fugitive adorer of the stationer's daughter was of a different stamp to his predecessors. He was one of a class—a gentleman by birth and position, and a prowler by profession. A prowler in fine clothes of fashionable cut, hanging about fashionable thoroughfares when London was in town, and going down to fashionable watering-places when London needed salt water. A man of the lynx order of bipeds, hunting for prey at all times and seasons, meeting with many rebuffs, and anon—and alas!—with sufficient encouragement—attracted by every fresh, innocent face; seeking it out as his profession; following it with a pertinacity that would have been creditable in any other pursuit—in fact, a scamp of the first water!

Harriet Wesden had gone westward in search of a book ordered by a customer, and had met this man, when homeward bound, in Regent Street. Harriet's face attracted him, and in a business-like manner, which told of long practice, he started in pursuit, regulating his conduct by the future manœuvres of the object in view. Harriet fluttered on her way homewards, conscious, almost by intuition, that she was followed; proceeding steadily in a south-eastern direction, and pertinaciously keeping the back of her straw bonnet to the pursuer. Had she looked behind once, our prowler would have increased his pace, and essayed to open a conversation—a half smile, even a look of interest, the ghost of an *œillade* would have been sufficient test of character for him, and he would have chanced his fortunes by a *coup d'étât.*

But he was in doubt. Once in crossing the Strand, towards Waterloo Bridge, he managed to veer round and confront her, but she never glanced towards him; so with a consideration not generally apparent in prowlers, he contented himself with following her home. He had his time on his hands—he had not met with an adventure lately—he was approaching a region that was not well known to him, and the smell of which disgusted him; but there was a something in Harriet Wesden's face which took him gingerly along, and he was a man who always followed his adventures to an end. Cool, calculating and daring, he would have made an excellent soldier—being brought up as an idler, he turned out a capital scoundrel.

Harriet reached her own door and gave a half timid, half inquiring glance round, before she passed into the shop; our prowler took stock of the name and the number—he had an admirable memory—examined everything in the shop window; walked on the opposite side of the way; looked up at the first and second floor, and met with nothing to reward his vigilance but the fierce face of old Hinchford; finally entered the shop and purchased some cigars, grinding his teeth quietly to himself over Mr. Wesden's suspicions of his sovereign being a counterfeit.

We should not have dwelt upon this incident, had it thus ended, or had no effect upon our story's progress. But, on the contrary, from the man's persistency, strange results evolved.

Twice or thrice a week this tall, high-shouldered, moustached *roué*, of five-and-thirty, appeared in Suffolk Street—patronized the bookseller's shop by purchases—hulked about street corners, watching the house, and catching a glimpse of Harriet occasionally. This was the Brighton romance over again, only Harriet was a year older now, and the hero of the story was sallow-faced and sinister—there was danger to any modest girl in those little scintillating eyes of his; and that other hero had been much younger, and had really loved her, she believed!

Pertinacity appears like devotion to some minds, and our prowler had met with his reward more than once by keeping doggedly to his post; he held his ground therefore, and watched his opportunity. Harriet Wesden had become frightened by this time; the adventure had lost its romantic side, and there was something in her new admirer's face which warned even her, a girl of no great penetration.

Mattie was always Harriet's *confidante* in these matters—Harriet was fond of asking advice how to proceed, although she did not always take the same with good grace. That little, black-eyed confidante kept watch in her turn upon the prowler, and resolved in her mind the best method of action.

"I'm afraid of him, Mattie," whispered Harriet; "I should not like father to know he had followed me home, lest he should think I had given the man encouragement, and father can be very stern when his suspicions are aroused. Besides, I shouldn't like Sidney to know."

"But he wouldn't believe that you had given him encouragement; he thinks too much of you, I fancy."

"You're full of fancies, Mattie."

"And—oh! there's the man again, looking under the *London Journals*. How very much like the devil in a French hat he is, to be sure!"

This dialogue occurred in the back parlour, whilst Mrs. Wesden was up-stairs, and Mr. Wesden in Paternoster Row in search of the December "monthlies"—and in the middle of it the devil in his French hat, stepped, with his usual cool imperturbability, into the shop.

This procedure always annoyed Mattie; she saw through the pretence, and, though it brought custom to the establishment, still it aggravated her. It was playing at shop, and "making-believe" to want something; and shop with our humble heroine was an important matter, and not to be lightly trifled with. She had her revenge in her way by selling the prowler the driest, hardest, and most undrawable of cigars, giving him the penny Pickwicks for the mild Havannahs; she sold him fusees that she knew had been left in a damp place, and the outside periodicals, which had become torn and soiled—could she have discovered a bad sixpence in the till, I believe, in her peculiar ideas of retaliation, she would not have hesitated an instant in presenting it, with his change.

The gentleman of energy entered the shop then, rolled his eyes over the parlour blind towards Harriet, who sat at fancy-work by the fireside, finally looked at Mattie, who stood stolidly surveying him. Now energy without a result had considerably damped the ardour of our prowler, and he had resolved to push a little forward in the sapping and mining way. He was a man who had made feminine pursuit a study; he knew human weakness, and the power of the money he carried in his pockets. He was well up in Ovid and in the old comedies of a dissolute age, where the Abigail is always tempted before the mistress—and Mattie was only a servant of a lower order, easily to be worked upon, he had not the slightest doubt. There was a servant who did the scrubbing of the stones before the door, and sat half out of window polishing the panes, till she curdled his blood, but she was a red-faced, stupid girl, and as there was a choice, he preferred that shop-girl, "with the artful black eyes," as he termed them.

"Good morning, Miss."

"Good morning."

"Have you any—any more of those exceedingly nice cigars, Miss?"

"Plenty more of them."

"I'll take a shilling's-worth."

Mattie, always anxious to get him out of the shop, rolled up his cigars in paper, and passed them rapidly across the counter. The prowler, not at all anxious, unrolled the paper, drew forth his cigar-case, and proceeded to place the "Havannahs" very carefully one by one in their proper receptacles, talking about the weather and the business, and even complimenting Mattie upon her good looks that particular morning, till Mattie's blood began to simmer.

"You haven't paid me yet, sir," she said, rather sharply.

"No, Miss—in one moment, if you will allow me."

After awhile, during which Mattie moved from one foot to another in her impatience, he drew forth a sovereign and laid it on the counter.

"We're short of change, sir—if you have anything smaller——"

"Nothing smaller, I am compelled to say, Miss."

Mattie hesitated. Under other circumstances, she would have left her shop, ran into the pork-butcher's next door, and procured change, after a hint to Harriet to look to the business; but she detected the *ruse* of the prowler, and was not to be outwitted. She opened her till again, and found fourteen shillings in silver—represented by a preponderance of threepenny pieces, but that was of no consequence, save that it took him longer to count—and from a lower drawer she drew forth one of many five-shilling packets of coppers, which pawnbrokers and publicans on Saturday nights were glad to give Mr. Wesden silver for, and laid it down with a heavy dab on the counter.

"What—what's that?" he ejaculated.

"That's ha'pence—that's all the change we've got—and I can't leave the shop," said Mattie, briskly. "You can give me my cigars back and get change for yourself, if you don't like it."

"Thank you," was the suave answer, "I was not thinking much about the change. If you will buy yourself a new bonnet with it, you will be conferring a favour upon me."

"And what favour will you want back?" asked Mattie, quickly.

"Oh! I will leave that to time and your kindness—come, will you take it and be friends with me? I want a friend in this quarter very much."

He pushed the silver and the cumbrous packet of coppers towards her. He was inclined to be liberal. He remembered how many he had dazzled in his time by his profuse munificence. Money he had never studied in his life, and by the strange rule of contraries, he had had plenty of it.

Mattie was impulsive—even passionate, and the effort to corrupt her allegiance to the Wesdens fired her blood to a degree that she even wondered at herself shortly afterwards.

"Take yourself out of this shop, you bad man," she cried, "and your trumpery change too! Be off with you before I call a policeman, or throw something at you—you great big coward, to be always coming here insulting us!"

With her impatient hands she swept the money off the counter, five-shilling packet of coppers and all, which fell with a crash, and disgorged its contents on the floor.

"What—what do you mean?" stammered the prowler.

"I mean that it's no good you're coming here, and that nobody wants to see you here again, and that I'll set the policeman on you next time you give me any of your impudence. Get out with you, you coward!"

Mattie thought her one threat of a policeman sufficient; she had still a great reverence for that official personage, and believed that his very name must strike terror to guilty hearts. The effect upon her auditor led her to believe that she had been successful; but he was only alarmed at Mattie's loud voice, and the stoppage of two boys and a woman at the door.

"I—I don't know what you mean—you're mad," he muttered, and then slunk out of the shop, leaving his cumbrous change for a sovereign spread over the stationer's floor. Mattie went round the counter and collected the *debris* of mammon, minus one threepenny piece which she could not discern anywhere, but which Mr. Wesden, toiling under his monthly parcel, detected in one corner immediately upon his entrance.

"Why, Mattie, what's this?—MONEY—*on the floor*!"

"A gentleman dropped his change, sir."

"Put it on the shelf, he'll be back for it presently."

"No, I don't think he will," was Mattie's dry response.

CHAPTER V.

PERSEVERANCE.

Mattie in her self-conceit imagined that she had frightened the prowler from Great Suffolk Street; in lieu thereof, she had only deterred him from entering a second appearance on the premises. He had made a false move, and reaped the bitter consequence. He must be more wary, if he built upon making an impression on Harriet Wesden's heart—more cautious, more of a strategist. So he continued to prowl at a distance, and to watch his opportunity from the same point of view. Presently it would come, and with the advantage of his winning tongue, which could roll off elegant phrases by the yard, he trusted to make an impression on a shopkeeper's daughter.

For a moment, and after his rebuff, he had hesitated as to the expediency of continuing the siege; but his pride was aroused; it was an unpleasant end to his plans, and the chance had not presented itself yet of trying his fortune with Miss Wesden herself. Presently the hour would come; he did not despair yet; he bided his time with great patience.

The time came a fortnight after that little incident in the Suffolk Street shop. Harriet Wesden was coming down the Borough towards home one wet night when he accosted her. It was getting late for one thing, and rainy for another, and Harriet was making all the haste home that she could, when he made her heart leap into her throat by his sudden "Good evening, Miss."

One glance at him, the nipping of a little scream in the bud, and then she increased her pace, the prowler keeping step with her.

"Will you favour me by accepting half my umbrella, Miss Wesden—for one instant then, whilst I venture to explain what may seem conduct the reverse of gentlemanly to you?"

"No, sir, I wish to hear nothing—I wish to be left alone."

"I have been very rude—I will ask your pardon, Miss Wesden, very humbly. But let me beg of you to listen to this explanation of my conduct."

"There is nothing to explain, sir."

"Pardon me, but there is. Pardon me, but this is not the way you would have treated Mr. Darcy had he been in my place."

Harriet gasped for breath. Mr. Darcy, the hero of her Brighton folly, the name which she had never confessed to a living soul, the only man in the world who she thought could have taunted her with indiscretion, and of being weak and frivolous rather than a rude and forward girl! Harriet did not reply; she looked at him closely, almost tremblingly, and then continued her hurried progress homewards; the prowler, seeing his advantage, maintained his position by her side, keeping the umbrella over her.

"Mr. Darcy was an intimate friend of mine before he went to India; we were together at Brighton, Miss Wesden—more than once he has mentioned your name to me."

"Indeed," she murmured.

"You would like to hear that he is well, perhaps."

"I am glad to hear that," Miss Wesden ventured to remark.

"He is in India still—I believe will remain there, marry and settle down there for good."

"Have you been watching my house to tell me this?"

"Partly, and partly for other reasons, for which I have a better excuse. I have been a wanderer—in search of happiness many years, and for the first time in a life not unadventurous there crosses my——"

"Good evening, sir—I have been entrapped into a conversation—I must beg you to leave me."

Harriet set off at the double again—in double quick time went the prowler after her.

People abroad that night began to notice the agitated girl, and the tall man marching on at her side, who, in his eagerness to keep step, trod on people's feet, and sent one doctor's boy, basket and bottles, crunching against a lamp-post; one or two stopped and looked after them and then continued their way—it was a race between the prowler and his victim, the prowler making a dead heat of it.

Harriet gave in at last—her spirit was not a very strong one, and she stopped and burst into tears.

"Sir, will you leave me?—will you believe that I don't want to hear a single word of your reasons for thus persecuting me?"

"Miss Wesden, only allow me to explain, and I will go my way and never see you more. I will vanish away in the darkness, and let all the bright hopes I have fostered float away on the current which bears you away from me."

"Go, pray do go, if you are a gentleman. I must appeal to some one for protection, if you——"

"Miss Wesden, you must hear me—you shall hear me. I am not a child; I am——"

"A scoundrel, evidently," said a harsh voice in his ears, and the instant afterwards Sidney Hinchford, with two fiery eyes behind his spectacles, stood between him and the girl he was persecuting. Harriet, with a little cry of joy, clung to the arm of her deliverer; the prowler looked perplexed, then put the best face upon the matter that he could extemporize for the occasion.

"Who are you, sir?" was the truly English expletive.

"My name is Hinchford—my address is at your service, if you wish it. Now, sir, your name—and *business*?"

"I decline to give it."

"You have insulted this lady, a friend of mine. Apologize," cried young Hinchford, in much such a tone as an irritable officer summons his company to shoulder arms.

"Sir, your tone is not calculated to induce me to oblige *you.* If Miss Wesden thinks that I——"

"APOLOGIZE!" shouted Hinchford, a second time. He had forgotten the respect due to his charge, and shaken her hand from his arm; he was making a little scene in the street, and convulsing Harriet with fright; he was face to face with the prowler, his tall, well-knit form, evidently a match for his antagonist; he was chivalrous, and scarcely twenty years of age; above all, he was in a towering passion, and verged a little on the burlesque, as passionate people generally do.

As if by the touch of a magic wand, a crowd sprang up around them; respectable passers-by, the pickets of the Kent Street gang on duty in the Borough, unwashed men and women who had been seeking shelter under shop-blinds, the doctor's boy, who had been maltreated and had a claim to urge for damages, a fish-woman, two tradesmen with their aprons on fresh from business, and shoals of boys who might have dropped from heaven, so suddenly did they take up the best places, and assume an interest in the adventure.

The prowler turned pale, and flinched a little as Sidney approached, flinched more as the audience seized the thread of discussion and expressed its comments more vociferously.

"Punch his head if he don't 'pologize, sir—throw him into the mud, sir—I'd cure him of coming after *my* gal—knock the bloke's hat off, and jump on it—lock him up!"

The prowler saw his danger; he had heard a great deal of the mercies of a London mob, and it was hemming him in now—and, like most men of the prowling class, he was at heart a coward. He succumbed.

"I never intended to insult the lady—if I have uttered a word to offend her, I am very sorry. It is all a misconception. But if the lady considers that I have taken a liberty in offering—in offering," he repeated, rather disturbed in his harangue by a violent shove from behind on to the unhappy doctor's boy, upon whose feet he alighted, "a common courtesy, I apologise with all my heart. I——"

"That will do, sir," was the curt response; "you have had a narrow escape. Take it as a lesson."

Sidney was glad to back out of the absurd position into which he had thrust Harriet, to draw her hand through his arm and hasten away, offering a a hundred excuses to her for his imprudence and impulsiveness.

He had not moved twenty yards with her when the yell of the mob—and the mob in that end of London possesses the finest blood-curdling yell in the world—startled him and all within half a mile of him. It was a dull night, and the wild elements of street life were fond of novelty; a swell had been caught insulting a British female in distress, and the unwashed hates swells like poison. An apology was not sufficient for the lookers-on; prostration on bended knees and hands outstretched would not have done; sackcloth and ashes vowed for the remainder of the delinquent's existence, would have been treated with contumely—all that was wanted was an uproar. The boys wanted an uproar because it was natural to them; the representatives of Kent Street, because it was in the way of trade, and one or two respectable gents had become interested in the dispute, and wore watch-chains; the women, because "*he* had not been sarved out as he desarved, the wretch!"

So the prowler, backing out of the crowd, met with a sledge-hammer hand upon his hat, and found his hat off, and mud in his face, and then fists, and finally an upheaving of the whole mass towards him, sending him into the roadway like a shell from an Armstrong gun. There was no help for it, the prowler must run, and run he did, pursued by the terrible mob and that more terrible yell which woke up every recess in the Borough; and in this fashion the pursuer and the pursued sped down the muddy road towards the Elephant and Castle.

An empty Hansom cab offered itself to the runaway; he leaped in whilst it was being slowly driven down the Borough, and dashed his fist through the trap.

"Drive fast—double fare—REFORM!"

The Hansom rattled off, the mob uttered one more despairing yell, and, after a slight abortive effort, gave up the chase, and left the prowler to his repentance.

And he did repent of mixing with life "over the water,"—for Great Suffolk Street never saw him again.

CHAPTER VI.

"IN THE FULNESS OF THE HEART," ETC.

"Oh! Harriet, I am very sorry," burst forth Sidney, when the noise had died away, and Harriet Wesden, pale and silent, walked on by his side with her trembling hand upon his arm.

Harriet did not reply—her dignity had been outraged, and his defence had not greatly assisted her composure, though it had answered the purpose for which it was intended.

Sidney gulped down a lump in his throat, and glanced at the pretty, agitated face.

"You are offended with me—well, I deserve it. I'm a beast."

This self-depreciatory verdict having consoled him, and elicited no response from Harriet, he continued, "I acted like a fool; I should have taken it coolly; why, he was more the gentleman of the two, scamp as he was. By George, I was near smashing him, though! Harriet," with eagerness, "you will look over my outburst. You're not so very much offended, are you?"

"No, I'm not offended, only the mob frightened me, and you were very violent. I don't know what else you could have done."

"Knocked him down and walked on, or given him in charge; knocked him down quietly would have been the most satisfactory method. How did it begin?"

"He followed and spoke to me. He has been hanging about the house for weeks."

"The dev—I beg pardon—has he though?"

Sidney Hinchford walked on; he had become suddenly thoughtful. More strongly than ever it recurred to him what a mistake he had made in not knocking down the prowler in a quiet and graceful manner.

"Mattie has noticed it, and spoken to him about it, but he would not go away."

"Did he ever speak to you before to-night."

"Never."

"He's a great blackguard!" Sidney blurted forth; "but there's an end of him. He'll not trouble you any more, Harriet; he did not know that you had a big brother to take care of you. These sorts of fellows object to big brothers—they're in the way so much."

"Yes, I suppose so."

"You oughtn't to go out at this time of night alone," he added after awhile; "it isn't exactly the thing, you know."

"No one spoke to me before."

"N—no, but it is not what *I* call proper."

"What you call proper, Mr. Hinchford!—I'm sure I—"

"I beg pardon; of course anything that I—I think proper, is of no consequence to you. It's only my way of speaking out—rather too plainly. I offend the clerks in the office at times and—and of course it's no business of mine, Harriet, although I did hope once that—that it would be. *There!*"

Harriet saw what was coming, or rather what had come. She was alarmed, although this was not her first offer, and the bloom of novelty had been lightly brushed off by that boarding-school folly of which she felt more ashamed every day. She began walking very fast, in much the same way from his passionate words as she had done from the frothy vapidity of that man, extinguished for ever.

Sidney walked on with her; her hand was sliding from his arm when he made a clutch at it, and held it rather firmly. He went at his love affairs in a straightforward manner—his earnestness making up for his lack of eloquence.

"I know I've done it!" he said; "I know I should have kept this back a year or two—perhaps altogether—but it wouldn't answer, and it has made me miserable, out of sorts, and an enigma to the old dad. I'm only just twenty—of no position yet, but with a great hope to make one—I'm sure that I shall love you all my life, and never be happy without you—can you put up with a fellow like me, and say I may hope to teach you to love me some day?"

A strange fear beset Harriet—a fear of answering before the whirl of events had given her time to consider. She had never seriously thought of pledging herself to him; though her woman's quickness had guessed at his secret long since, she had never dreamed of him or felt her heart beat for him, as for that first love who had won her girl's fancy, and then faded away like a dream-figure. She was agitated from the preceding events of that night, and now, in an unlucky moment, he added to her embarrassment and made her brain whirl—she was scarcely herself, and did not answer like herself.

"Let go my hand, sir—let me go home—I don't want to hear any more!"

"Very well," he answered; and was silent the rest of the way home—leaving her without a word in the shop, and passing through that side door reserved for the Hinchfords for the last thirteen years. Harriet, trembling and excited, almost stumbled into the back parlour, and began to sob forth a part of the adventures of that evening. Sidney, like the ghost of himself, stalked into the first-floor front, where his father was keeping a late tea for him.

The anxious eyes of the father glanced from under the bushy white brows; he was a student of human nature, so far as his son was concerned at least.

"Anything wrong, Sid?"

"N—no," was the hesitative answer.

"You look troubled."

"I'm tired—dead beat."

"Let us get on with the tea, then," he said assuming a cheery voice; "here's the *Times*, Sid."

"I have read it," was the hollow answer.

"Oh! I haven't—any news?"

"Tea gone up with a rush, I believe."

"Ah! good for the firm, I hope."

"Believe so—don't know. Phew! how infernally hot this room gets!"

Mr. Hinchford hazarded no more remarks—the curt replies of his son were sufficient indication of a reluctance to attend to him. He set out the tea-table, and superintended the duties thereof in a grave, fatherly manner, glancing askance at his son over the rim of his tea-cup. Sidney was in a mood that troubled the sire—for it was an unusual mood, and suggested something very much out of the way.

After tea, Sidney would compose himself and relate what had happened in the City to disturb him, and led him to respond churlishly to the old father, who had never given him a cross word in his life. He would wait Sidney's good time—there was no good hurrying the lad.

These two were something more than father and son; their long companionship together, unbroken upon by other ties, had engendered a concentrative affection which was a little out of the common—which more resembled in some respects the love existent between a good mother and daughter. They were friends, confidants, inseparable companions as well. The son's ambition was the father's, and all that interested and influenced the one equally affected the other. Sidney had made no friends from the counting-house or warehouse clerks; they were not "his sort," and he shunned their acquaintance. He was a young man of an unusual pattern, a trifle more grave than his years warranted, and endued with more forethought than the whole business put together. He looked at life sternly—too sternly for his years—and his soul was absorbed in rising to a good position therein, for his father's sake as well as his own. His father was growing old; his memory was not so good as it used to be; Sid fancied that the time would shortly come when the builders would discover his father's defects, dismiss him with a week's salary, and find a younger and sharper man to supply his place. That was simply business in a commercial house; but it was death to the incapables, whom sharp practice swept out of the way. Sidney felt that he had no time to lose; that there must come a day when his father's position would depend upon himself; when he should have to work for both, as his father had worked for him when he was young and helpless and troublesome. Sidney's employers were kind, more than that, they were deeply interested in the strange specimen of a young man who worked hard, objected to holidays, and took work home with him when there was a pressure on the firm; he was honest, energetic and truthful, and a servant with those requisites is always worth his weight in gold. They had conferred together, and resolved to make a partner of him in due course, when he was of age or when he was five-and-twenty; and Sidney, though he had never been informed of their intentions, guessed it by some quick instinct, read it in their faces, and believed that good luck would fall to his share some day. Still he never spoke of his hopes, save once to his father in a weak moment, of which he ever after repented, for his father was of a more sanguine nature, and inclined to build his castles too rapidly. Sidney knew the uncertainties of life—more especially of city life—and he proceeded quietly on his way, keeping his hopes under pressure, and talking and thinking like a clerk in the City who never expected to reach higher than two or three hundred a year.

Yet with all his prudence he was, singular to relate, not of a reticent nature; he was a young man who spoke out, and hated mystery or suspense.

Possibly in this last instance he had spoken out too quickly for Harriet Wesden; and though suspense was over, he did not feel pleased with his tactics of that particular evening. And he *was* inclined to keep back all the unpleasant reminiscences of that night, sink them for ever in the waters of oblivion, and never let a soul know what an ass he had made of himself. It was his first imprudence, and he was aggrieved at it; he had given way to impulse, and suffered his love to escape at an unpropitious moment—his ears burned to think of all the folly which he had committed.

In a bad temper—he who was generally so calm and equable—he took his tea, and shunned his father's inspection by turning his back upon him. After a while he took up the *Times*, which he had previously declined, and feigned an interest in the "Want Places." Mattie came in and out of the room with the hot water, &c.; she waited on the Hinchfords when Ann of all work was weak in the ankles, which was of frequent occurrence. Mattie made herself generally useful, and rather liked trouble than not. With a multiplicity of tasks on her mind, she was always more cheerful; it was only when there was nothing to do that her face assumed a sternness of expression as if the shadow of her early days were settling there.

Mattie, bustling to and fro in attendance upon the Hinchfords, observed all and said nothing, like a sensible girl. She was quick enough to see that something unusual had happened above stairs as well as below, and her interest was as great in these two friends—and *helpers*—as in the Wesdens. She would have everybody happy in that house—it had been a lucky house for her, and it should be for all in it, if she possessed the power to make it so!

She saw that one trouble had come at least; and looking intently at Sidney's grim face—she had busied herself with the bread and butter plate to get a good look at it—she read its story more plainly than he would have liked.

Outside the door she paused and put "this and that together"—*this* in the drawing-room, and *that* in the parlour, and jumped at once at the right conclusion, with a rapidity that did infinite credit to her seventeen years. Seventeen years then, and rather shorter than ever, if that were possible.

"He has been courting Harriet—I know he has!" she said; "and Harriet's been in a tantrum, and said something to cross him—that's it!"

She missed a step and shook up the tea-things that she was carrying down-stairs. This recalled her to the duties of her situation.

"One thing at a time, Mattie, my dear," she said, in a patronizing way to herself, as she descended to the lower regions. In those lower regions poor Ann Packet created another divergence of thought. Ann's ankles continued to swell—she had been much on her feet during the last heavy wash, and the gloomy thought had stolen to her, that her new calamity—she was a woman born for calamities—would end in the hospital.

This idea having just seized her, she communicated it at once to Mattie, upon her re-appearance in the kitchen.

"Mattie," said Ann, lugubriously, "I've been a good friend to you, all my life—ain't I?"

"To be sure you have," was the quick answer.

"When you came here first, a reg'lar young rip, I took to you, taught you what was tidiness, which you didn't know any more than the babe unborn, did you?"

"Not much more—don't you feel so well to-night, Ann?"

"Much wus—I'm only forty, and my legs oughtn't to go at that age."

"No, and they won't."

"*Won't* they?" was the ironical answer; "but they will—but they has! Oh! Mattie gal, you'll come and see me at St. Tummas's?"

"Ann Packet," said Mattie gravely, "this won't do. You're getting your old horrors again, and you're full of fancies, and your ankles are not half so bad as you think they are. I know what *you* want."

"What?"

"A good shaking," laughed Mattie, "that's all."

"Oh! you unnat'ral child!"

"Well, the unnat'ral child will ask Mr. Wesden if she may keep out of the shop to-night, and bring a book down-stairs to read to you, over your needlework. But if you don't work I shan't read, Ann—is it a bargain?"

"You're allus imperent; but get the book, if master'll let you. Oh! how *they* do shoot!"

Mattie obtained permission, brought down a book from the store, and sat down to read to honest Ann. She had made a good choice, and Ann was soon interested, forgot her ailments, and stitched away with excitable rapidity. Mattie had no time for thoughts of her own, or the new mystery above-stairs till the supper hour. She read on till the Hinchford bell rang once more; then she closed the book, and met with her reward in Ann's large red hand falling heavily, yet affectionately, on her shoulder.

"Thankee, Mattie. I'll do as much for you some day, gal."

"When you can spell, or when I've gouty ankles, Ann?"

"Ah! get out with you!—I'm only fit for making game on, you think. I'm a poor woman, who never had the time to larn to read, and the likes of you can laugh at me."

"No—only try to make you laugh, Ann. You're not cross?"

"God bless you!—not I," she ejaculated spasmodically. "There, go about your work, and don't think anything of what an old fool like me talks about."

Mattie busied herself with the supper tray, the bread, cheese, knives and plates, and then bore them away in her strong arms; Ann watched her out of the room, and then produced an indifferently clean cotton handkerchief, with which she wiped her eyes and blew her nose.

"To think how that gal has altered since she first came here, a little ragged thing," soliloquized Ann, "a gal who skeered you with the wulgar words she'd picked up in the streets, and was so awful ignorant, you blushed for her. And now the briskiest and best of gals; if I don't spend all my money in doctors stuff afore I die, that Mattie shall have every penny of it. It's in my will so; they put it down in black and white for me, and she'll never know it till I'm—I'm gone!"

A prospect that caused Ann Packet to weep afresh; a dismal, but a soft-hearted woman, who had passed through life with no one to love, until she met with the stray. She was a stray herself, picked up at the workhouse gate, to the disgust of the relieving officer, and turned out to service as soon as she could walk and talk, and a mistress be found for her—lonely in the world herself, she had, when the time came round, taken to one more forlorn and friendless than ever she had been. And she *had* left her all her money—fourteen pounds, seven and sevenpence, put out at interest, two and seven eighths, in the Finsbury Savings Bank, whither her ankles refused to carry her to get her book made up, another trouble at that time which kept her mind unsettled.

CHAPTER VII.

CONFIDENCE.

Whilst Mattie read to her fellow-workman, consolation was also being attempted in the drawing-room that she had quitted. Consolation attempted by the father after awhile to his son.

After awhile, for an hour passed before a word was exchanged, and Sidney Hinchford still held the newspaper before him, staring at it, without comprehending a word. A singular position for him to adopt; a youth of twenty, who never wasted time, who had always something on his hands to fill up his evenings at home, who was very often too busy to play backgammon with his father.

That father was troubled; his heart was in his son's peace of mind; there was nothing that he would not have sacrificed for it, had it lain in his power. His pride was in his son's advancement, his son's ability, and he fancied that a great trouble had occurred at the business to change the scene in which both played their parts. He was less strong-minded and more nervous than he had been four years ago, and so less affected him.

When the hour had passed, and he had grown tired of Sidney's silence, he said, with something of his son's straightforwardness,

"What's the matter, Sid?"

Sidney crumpled the paper in his hands, and flung it on the table; he was tired, even a little ashamed of his sullen deportment.

"A matter that I ought to keep to myself, it being a foolish one, sir," he answered; "but, if you wish, I will relate it."

"If *you* wish, Sid," was the courteous answer; "I have no wish to hear anything that you would desire to keep back from me. If you think I can be of no use to you, give you no advice, offer no consolation that you may think worthy of acceptance, and if," with a very wistful glance towards him, "you consider it a matter that concerns yourself alone, why I—I don't wish to intrude upon your confidence."

"I don't think that we have had any secrets from each other yet; I don't see any reason why we should begin to get mysterious, father," Sidney replied; "and so, here's the full, true, and particular account."

Mr. Hinchford edged his chair nearer to his son, the son turned and looked his father in the face, blushing just a little at the beginning of his narrative.

"It's an odd thing for one *man* to tell another," he said quickly, "but it's what you ought to know, and though it makes me wince a little, it's soon over. I've been thinking of engaging myself to——"

"Not to another firm, Sid—*now*?" cried the father, as he paused.

"To Harriet Wesden, down-stairs."

"God bless me!"

Mr. Hinchford passed his hands through his scanty white hairs, stroked his moustache, blew at an imaginary something in the air, loosened his stock, and gasped a little. His son engaging himself to be married was a new element to perplex him; he had never believed in human nature, or the Hinchford nature, taking that turn for years and years. Once or twice he had thought that his careful son might some day look around him and *marry well*; but that at twenty years of age he should have fallen in love, was a miracle that took some minutes to believe in.

"Well," he said at last.

"I should have said, father, that I had been thinking of an engagement—a long one to end in a happy marriage, when there was fair sailing for all of us—and that my thoughts found words when I least expected them, and surprised Harriet by their suddenness. I told her I loved her, and she told me that she didn't—and there's an end of it! We need not speak of the affair again, you know."

"'And that she didn't!'" quoted the father, "why, that's more amazing still!"

"On the contrary, that is the most natural part of it."

"And she really said—"

"She said that she did not want any more of my jaw—rather more elegantly expressed, but that is what she meant. Well, I *was* a fool!"

Mr. Hinchford sat and reflected, becoming graver every instant. He did not attempt to make light of the story, to treat it as one of those trifles 'light as air,' which a breath would disperse. His son's was neither a frivolous nor a romantic nature, and he treated even his twenty years with respect. Mr. Hinchford was astonished also at his own short-sightedness; the strangeness of this love passage darting across the monotony of his quiet way, without a flash from the danger signal by way of hint at its approach. He saw how it was to end, very clearly now, he thought; Harriet Wesden and his son would contract an early engagement, marry in haste, and cut him off by a flank movement, from his son's society. He saw the new loves replacing the old, and himself, white-haired and feeble, isolated from the boy to whom his heart yearned. He scarcely knew how he had idolized his son, until the revelation of this night. Still he was one of the least selfish men in the world; Sidney's happiness first, and then the thought how best to promote his own.

After a few more questions and answers, Mr. Hinchford mastered the position of affairs. Harriet Wesden loved his boy—that was a certainty, and to be expected—and her timid embarrassment at Sid's sudden proposal, and her nervous escape from it, were but natural in that sex which poor Sid knew so little concerning. And the Wesdens, *père et mère*, why, they would be proud of the match; for Sid's abilities would make a gentleman of him, and Sid in good time—all in good time—would raise the stationer's daughter to a position, of which she might well be proud! He liked the Wesdens, but heigho!—he had looked forward to his boy doing better in the world, finding a wife more suitable for him in the future.

It was all plain enough, but he furbished up his philosophy, nevertheless—that odd philosophy which at variance with his brighter thoughts, sought to prepare those to whom it appealed for the worst that might happen. He looked at the worst aspect of things, whilst his heart had not a doubt of the best; he would have prepared all the world for the keenest disappointments, and been the man to give way most, and to be the most astounded at the result, had his prophecies come true. Years ago he foretold Mattie's ingratitude and duplicity in return for his patronage; but he had not believed a word of his forebodings. He had told his son not to build upon so improbable a thing as a partnership with his employers at so early an age; but he was more feverishly expectant than his son, and so positive that his son's abilities would be thus rewarded, that his pride had expanded of late years, and he talked more like the rich man he had been once himself.

Mr. Hinchford prepared his son for the worst that evening; and the son, knowing his character, felt a shadow removed at every dismal conjecture as to how the little love affair would terminate.

"You can't let it rest here, however bad it may turn out, Sid."

"No, of course not."

"You must see Harriet's father in the morning, and make a clean breast of it; and then if he turn you off with a short word—feeling himself a rich man, and above the connection—why, you will put up with it gravely, and like a Hinchford. There are a great many things against your chances, my boy."

"We're both too young, perhaps," suggested Sidney, more dolefully.

"Years too young," was the reply; "and people have unpleasant habits of changing their minds—and then what a fix it would be, Sid! Why, Harriet Wesden's not eighteen till next month—quite a child!"

"No, I'm hanged if she is!" burst forth Sidney.

"Well then, you're but a boy, after all; and these long and early engagements are bad things for both. But still as it has come, you must speak to the old people; and if they have no objection—which I think they will have—and Harriet is inclined to accept you—which I think she isn't—why, make the best of it, work on in the old sure and steady fashion—you're worth waiting for, my lad."

"Thank you, dad," was the reply; "you're very kind, but your opinion of me is not the world's. I'm a cross-grained, unforgiving, disagreeable person—there!"

"In your enemy's estimation—but your friends?"

"I don't know that I have any."

"Oh! we shall see—and if you have not any abroad," he added, "you must put up with the old one at home, Sid."

"He will put up with me, I hope; he will remember that I have only him yet awhile to tell my hopes and fears to, standing in the place of the mother."

"Ah! the good mother, lost so early to us!—she should have heard this story, Sid."

The old man snatched up the paper and began reading; the son turned to his own work at last, and was soon buried in accounts. But the paper was uninteresting, and the accounts foggy; after awhile both gave it up, and talked again of the old subject. Sid's full heart overflowed that night, and his reticence belonged not to it; he was sure of sympathy with his feelings, and had the mother—ever a gentle and dear listener—been at his side, he could not have more fully dwelt upon the love which had troubled him so long, and which he had kept so well concealed. It had grown with his growth; Harriet's playfellow, Harriet's brother, finally Harriet's lover. Page after page, chapter after chapter of the story which begins ever the same, and only darts off at a tangent when the crisis, such as his, comes in due course, to end in various ways—happily, deplorably—in the sunshine of comedy, the mystery of melodrama, the darkness of tragedy, taking its hues from the "surroundings," and giving us poor scribes no end of subjects to write upon.

Mr. Hinchford was a patient listener; other men might have been wearied by the romantic side to a love-sick youth's character; but Sid was a part of himself, and he had no ambition, no hope in which his son did not stand in the foreground, a bright figure to keep him rejoicing.

Supper served and over, Sidney retired to his share in the double-bedded room at the back—the shabby room with which Mr. Hinchford had lately grown disgusted, and even wished to quit, knowing not his son's reason for remaining—leaving the father to fill his after-supper pipe before the fire. Mr.

Hinchford was in a reflective, wide-awake mood, and not inclined for rest just then; he sat with his slippered feet on the fender, puffing away at his meerschaum. Had he not promised his son to keep away from Mr. Wesden until the *dénouement* had been brought about by Sid's own method, he would have gone down stairs and talked it over with the old people; but the promise given, he would sit there and think of his son's chances, and pray for them, as they were nearest his heart then.

He was a father who understood human nature a little, not so much as he fancied himself, but who was, nevertheless, a man of discernment, when his simple vanity did not stand in the way.

He had not thought deeply of Harriet Wesden before; now that there loomed before him the prospect of calling her "daughter," he conjured up every reminiscence connected with her, and set himself to think whether such a girl were likely to make Sid happy, or to love Sid as that pure-hearted, honest lad deserved. He was astonished, after a while, at the depth of his researches into the past; he could remember her a light-hearted child, a vivacious girl, now, presto, a woman, whom Sid sought for a wife; he could see her flitting before him, a pretty girl, swayed a little by the impulse of the hour, and verging on extremes; he called to mind certain traits of character that had struck him more than once, and had then been forgotten in the hurrying passage of events foreign to her; he sat studying an abstruse volume, and perplexing himself with its faintly written characters. Mothers have had such thoughts, and made them the business of a life, sorrowing and rejoicing over them, and praying for their children's future; seldom fathers, before whom are ever the counting-house in the City, the bargains to be made in the mart or on the exchange, the accommodation to be had at the bankers'.

Hinchford thought like a woman; he was a clerk whose business thoughts ended when he came home at night, and he was alone in the world with one hope. All the old worldly thoughts lay apart from him, and the affections of paternity were stronger within him in consequence. He lived for Sid, not for himself.

He was still in a brown study, when the shuffling feet of Mrs. Wesden, being assisted up-stairs by her husband to the top back room, disturbed him for an instant; then the rustle of a dress, and the light footfall of the daughter, assured him of Harriet's retirement. All was still in that crowded house which he had wished to exchange a year ago for a house in the suburbs, suitable to the united salaries of himself and boy. He thought of that wish, and sighed to think it had not been carried out, for, after all, he was not quite satisfied with the turn affairs had taken.

The door opened suddenly and startled his nerves. He turned a scared face towards the intruder, who jumped a little at the sight of him sitting before the grate, black, yawning and uninviting at that hour.

"I thought you had gone, Mr. Hinchford," said Mattie; "I came for the supper tray and to tidy up a bit here, and save time in the morning."

"How's Ann?" he asked absently.

"Better, I think," replied Mattie, still standing at the door.

"You can clear away—I'm going in a minute. How's the evening school, girl?"

"Why, I have left it this twelvemonth!"

"To be sure—I had forgotten that you had learned all that they could teach you, and had become too much of a woman. Why, we shall hear of you being married next."

"Who's going to be married *now—Mr. Sidney*?"

"Confound you! how sharp you are," said Mr. Hinchford a little dismayed; "no, I never said so—mind I never said a word, so don't let us have any ridiculous tattling."

"I never tattle," said Mattie in an offended tone. "Oh! Mr. Hinchford," she added suddenly, "you can always trust *me* with anything."

"I hope so, Mattie—I hope so."

"And if Mr. Sidney thinks of marrying our Harriet, you may trust me not to let the people round here know a word about it. Not a word, sir!" she repeated, with pursed lips.

Mr. Hinchford ran his hands through his hair, and loosened his stock again. He was confused, he had betrayed his hand, and made a mess of it, or else Mattie knew more than he gave her credit for, it was doubtful which.

"Mattie," he said, after a while, when that young woman, rapid in her movements, had packed the tray and was proceeding to retire with it.

"Yes, sir."

She left the table and came nearer to him.

"Whatever made you think that my dear boy was likely to—to take a fancy to Harriet?"

"I've noticed that he talks to her a good deal, and comes into the back parlour a great deal, and brightens up when she speaks to him, and you can see his eyes dancing away behind the little spectacles he's taken to—and very becoming they are, sir."

"Very," asserted the old gentleman.

"And he's always dull when she's out, and fidgets till he knows where she has gone, and tries to make me tell; and so I've fancied, oh! ever so long, that Harriet and he would make a match of it some day."

He was amazed at this girl ascertaining the truth before himself, but he retained his cool demeanour.

"Some long day hence, mayhap—who can tell?"

"Love's as uncertain as life—isn't it, sir?"

"Ahem—yes."

"At least, I've read so," corrected Mattie. "It's a thing I shall never understand, Mr. Hinchford."

"Time enough—time enough, my girl."

"But our Harriet, she's pretty, she's a lady, she's meant to be loved by everybody she meets, and she's the only one that's good enough to marry *him*."

She lowered her voice at the last word, and made a quick movement with her hand in the direction of the adjoining room.

"You are very fond of Harriet, Mattie?" said Mr. Hinchford, curiously.

"As I need be, sir, surely."

"Ah! surely—she is amiable and kind."

"Always so, I think."

"A little thoughtless, perhaps—eh?"

He was curious concerning Harriet Wesden now—no match-making mother could have taken more indirect and artful means to elicit the truth concerning her child's elect.

"Why, that's it!" exclaimed Mattie; "that's why Mr. Sidney ought to marry her."

"Oh! is it?"

"You'll see, sir," said Mattie, suddenly drawing a chair close to Mr. Hinchford, and assuming a position on the edge thereof; "you'll soon see, sir, what I mean by that."

"Yes—yes."

It was a strange picture, with an odd couple in the foreground; Harriet Wesden, Sidney Hinchford, or afflicted Ann Packet, coming in suddenly, would have been puzzled what to make of it. The burlesque side to the scene did not strike Mr. Hinchford till long afterwards; the slight figure of the girl on the chair before him, the rapid manner in which she expounded her theory, her animation, sudden gestures, and, above all, his own intense interest in the theme, and forgetfulness of the confidence he placed in her by his own absorbent *pose.* He had put his pipe aside, and, open-mouthed and round-eyed, was drinking in every word, clutching his knees with his hands, meanwhile.

"Mr. Sidney isn't thoughtless. He's careful, and he has a reason for everything, and he will keep her from harm all her life. She'll be the best and brightest of wives to him, if they should ever marry, which I do hope and pray they will, sir, soon. I'm sure there are no two who would make a happier couple, and oh!—to see them happy," clapping her hands together, "what would *I* give!"

"You haven't lost your interest in us, then, Mattie?"

"When I forget the prayers that Mrs. Wesden taught me, or the first words of yours that set me thinking that I might grow good, or all the kindness which everybody in this house has shown for me, then I shall lose that, sir—not before!"

"You're an uncommon girl, Mattie."

"No, sir."

"You show an uncommon phase—great gratitude for little kindnesses. I'm glad to see this interest in Harriet and my boy—perhaps they might do worse than make a match of it. But—but," suddenly returning to the subject which engrossed him, "hasn't it struck you—just a little, mind, nothing to speak of—that Harriet Wesden is a trifle vain?"

"Wouldn't you be proud of your good looks, if you had any?" was the sharp rejoinder.

"Um," coughed he, "I daresay I might."

"I should be always staring at myself in the glass if I had her complexion, her golden hair, her lovely blue eyes. I should be proud to think that my pretty face had made my happiness by bringing the thoughts of such a son as yours to me."

"Ah! I didn't see it in that light," said he, tugging at his stock again, "and I—I daresay everything will turn out for the best. We will not dwell upon this any more, but let things take their course, and not spoil them by interference, or by talking about them, Mattie."

"Don't fear me," said Mattie, rising.

"I don't think it is our place," he added, associating himself with Mattie, to render his hints less personal, "to be curious about it, and seek to pry into what is going on in the hearts of these young people. Do you think now, Mattie, that she's inclined to be fond of—of my Sid?"

"I don't say she'd own it just now—but I think she is. Why shouldn't she be?"

"Ah!—why, indeed. There's not a boy like him in the whole parish."

"No, sir."

"And Harriet Wesden will be a lucky girl."

"Ah! that she will!"

"And—and now good night, Mattie, and the less we repeat of this gossip the better."

"Certainly—things had better take their course without *our* interference."

"Yes," was the dry answer.

Mattie seized her tray, and prepared to depart. At the door, with her burden *en avance* she paused, went back to the table, replaced her tray, and returned to Mr. Hinchford's side.

"Something happened to-night! The dear girl has been disturbed—I hope Mr. Sidney has not been in a hurry, and——"

"Hush! I don't think he's asleep. Good night—good night."

"When *she* was a year younger, it was hard work to keep back what was in her heart from me; but she's growing older in her ways, and better able to understand that I'm only a poor servant, after all. I don't complain," said Mattie, "she's always kind and good to me, but she's my mistress's daughter, rather than the sister—or something like the sister—that used to be. And I do so like to know everything, sir!"

"So it seems," remarked Mr. Hinchford.

"Everything that concerns her, I mean—because I might be of help when she least expected it. And so Mr. Sidney has told her all about it to-night?"

"I never said so," cried the embarrassed old gentleman.

"Well, I only guess at it," answered Mattie; "I shall soon come to the rights of it, if I keep a good look out."

She caught up her tray again and marched to the door to ponder anew. Mr. Hinchford writhed on his chair—would this loquacious diminutive help never go down-stairs and leave him in peace? She asked no more questions, however.

"And to think that what I fancied would happen is all coming round like a story-book, just as I hoped it would be for her sake—for his sake—years and years ago! How nicely things come round, sir, don't they?"

"Don't they!" he re-echoed.

Mattie departed, and the old gentleman blew at invisibility in the air once more.

"How that girl does talk!—it is her one fault—loquacity. If she can only find a listener, she's happy. And yet, when I come to consider it, that girl's always happy—for she's thankful and content. And things are coming nicely round, she says—well, I hope so!"

CHAPTER VIII.

SIDNEY STATES HIS INTENTIONS.

Mr. Wesden, if not the first person up in the house, was at least the first person who superintended business in the morning. For years that little shop had been opened punctually at six A.M. When the boy had not arrived to take down the shutters, Mr. Wesden lowered them himself. Tradesfolk over the way, early mechanics sallying forth to work from the back streets adjacent, the policeman on duty, the milkboy, and the woman with the watercresses, knew when it was six o'clock in Great Suffolk Street by the opening of Mr. Wesden's shop.

Mr. Wesden prided himself upon this punctuality, and not even to Mattie would he entrust the duties of commencing the labours of the day, despite the inflexibility of his back after a night's "*rest.*"

Sidney Hinchford, who knew Mr. Wesden's habits, therefore found no difficulty in meeting with that gentleman at five minutes past the early hour mentioned.

"Good morning, Mr. Wesden."

"Good morning, Sidney."

Mr. Wesden was sitting behind his counter, in business position, ready for customers; the morning papers had not come in from the agent—he had given up of late years fetching them from the office himself—and there was not much to distract him from full attention to all that Sidney had to communicate.

"I thought I should find you handy for a serious bit of talk, sir."

Mr. Wesden looked at him, and his face assumed a degree of extra gravity. Sidney Hinchford had got into debt with his tailor, and wished to borrow a few pounds "on the quiet."

"I suppose Harriet told you last night what happened?"

"Not all that happened, I fancy."

"Then she waited for me, possibly," he said, a little taken aback nevertheless, "or told her mother. Well, you see, to make a long story short, Mr. Wesden, I have taken the liberty of falling in love with your daughter, as was natural and to be expected, and I have come down early this morning to tell you plainly that that's the state of my feelings, and that if you have anything to say against it or me, why you can clap on the extinguisher, and no one a bit the wiser."

Mr. Wesden was a man who never showed his surprise by anything more than an intenser stare than usual; he sat looking stolidly at Sidney Hinchford, who leaned over the counter with flushed cheeks and earnest eyes, surveying him through his glasses.

Still Mr. Wesden was surprised—in fact, very much astonished. Only a year or two ago, and the tall young man before him was a little boy fresh from school, and a source of trouble to him when he got near the tinsel drawer, and Skelt's Scenes and Characters—now he was talking of love matters.

"You're the first customer this morning, Sidney, and you've asked for a rum article," he said bluntly.

"Which you'll not refuse me, I hope, sir—which you'll give me a chance of obtaining, at all events."

"What does Harriet say?"

"I've—I've only just said a few words to her—more than I ought to have said perhaps, before I know her feelings towards me, or what your wishes were, sir."

Sidney, very humble and deferential to pater-familias, after taking the case in his own hands, like all young hypocrites who have this terrible ordeal to pass, and are doubtful of the upshot.

Mr. Wesden listened and stared—clean over Sidney's head, rather than at him. Had he not had a long experience of the stationer's ways, he would have augured ill for his prospects from the stolidity with which his news was received; but Mr. Wesden was always a grave and reserved man, and his immobile features did not alarm the young suitor.

"Well, and what's to keep her and you—*my money*?"

"Not a farthing of it, sir, by your good leave," said Sidney, proudly; "I wish to work on and wait for her. I have every hope of attaining to a good position in my office—I think I see my way clearly—I won't ask you to let her marry me till I can show you a home of my own, and a little money in the bank, sir."

"Why didn't you wait till then?" was the dry question.

"Why, because a fellow wants a hope to live on—permission from you to pay his addresses to Miss Harriet, and to ask her to give me a hope too."

"I see."

Mr. Wesden fidgeted about his top drawers, folded some papers, looked in his till, and then turned his little withered face to Sidney. The face had altered, was brighter, even wore a smile, and Sidney's heart leaped again.

"If you'd been like most young men, I should have said 'Not yet.' But you haven't crept about the bush, and you've dealt fair, and I'll promise all I can without tying the girl up too closely."

"Tying her up!"

"The home of your own hasn't turned up yet," shrewdly remarked the stationer; "and though I believe that and the money will, we may as well wait for some signs of them. And——"

"Well, well."

"Don't you be in a hurry, young man; breath don't come so fast as it did, and I'm not used to long speeches."

"Take your time, sir—I beg pardon."

"And Harriet's very young, and may see some one else to like better."

"I hope not, sir."

"And *you* are very young, and may see some one else too."

"Oh! Mr. Wesden."

"Ah! it's shocking to think of, but these awful events do occur," said the old man, satirically; "and, besides, my old lady and I are ignorant people in one way, and mayn't suit you when you get bigger and prouder."

"Mr. Wesden, you'll not fancy that, I know."

"You'll have to think whether, when you are a great man, you'll be able to put up with the old lady and me coming to see our girl sometimes."

Sidney entered another protest—was prolific, even liberal in his invitations, which he issued on the spot.

"Then if it's not an engagement, or what I call downright keeping company just yet—say for another year at least, I shan't turn my back upon you."

"Thank you, sir—you are more than generous."

He leaned across the counter and shook hands with Mr. Wesden; the news-agent drove up in his pony-cart at the same moment, and directly afterwards had flung a heavy bundle of the "early mornings" upon the counter; the news-boy entered, and waited for orders for his first round; a little girl came in for a penny postage stamp, change for sixpence, and a piece of paper to wrap the lot in. Business was beginning in Great Suffolk Street, and Sidney Hinchford getting in the way. Sidney would have liked to add a little more, but Mr. Wesden stopped him.

"Harriet's been down this half hour," he said; "I suppose you know that."

"Indeed I did not, sir," exclaimed Sidney, with a wild glance towards the parlour.

Harriet was there, busying herself with the breakfast cloth—a domestic picture, fair and glowing. He dashed into the parlour, and Harriet, prepared for him now, listened demurely, felt her heart plunging a little, but did not rebuke him with any words similar to those of yesternight. His despairing look of that period had kept her restless all night; she could not bear to know that others were unhappy, and she fancied that she should soon learn to love him, if she did not love him already, for his manliness and frankness. So she listened, and Sidney detailed his interview with her father, and her father's wish that it should not be considered an engagement between them until at least another year had passed.

"We are to go on just the same as if nothing had happened, but—but I wish you to look forward to the end of that year like myself, to have hope in me and my efforts, and to give me hopes of you."

"Am I worth hoping for, Sidney?" was the rejoinder; "you don't know half the foolishness of which I have been guilty—what a weak, frivolous, romantic girl I have been."

She thought of her Brighton romance, opened the book, and then shut it hastily again. It was a story he had no right to know yet, and she had not the courage to tell him just then—it belonged wholly to the past, so rake the dead leaves over it and let it rest again!

Let it rest, then; there was no engagement. Both were free to change their minds before the year was out in which the strength of their love would be put to the test. For that year nothing more than friends, she thought, or a something more than friends, and less than lovers.

The half bargain was concluded, and Sidney went on his way rejoicing. There was rejoicing in the hearts of all in that house for a while. Mrs. Wesden cried over her girl as though she was going away to-morrow, but talked as if it were a settled engagement, and was glad that Sidney Hinchford was to be her son-in-law some day. Mr. Hinchford and Mr. Wesden smoked their pipes together that evening, and talked about it in short disjointed sentences, amidst which Mr. Hinchford learned that Mr. Wesden would retire from business before the year's probation had expired, leaving Mattie, possibly, in charge. Mattie and Ann Packet in the lower regions dwelt upon the same subject, free debatable ground, which no one cared to hem round by restrictions.

Late in the evening, Mattie stole up to Harriet's bed-room, and knocked softly at the panels of the door.

"May I come in?" she asked.

"To be sure, Mattie."

"I thought that you would be sitting here, thinking of it."

"Thinking of what, Mattie?"

"Ah! you don't tell me anything now—but I can guess—and Mr. Sidney did not sit in the parlour all the evening for nothing!"

"No, Mattie; but it's not a downright engagement yet. I'm to try if I can like Sidney first."

"That's the best way—didn't I say that this would happen some day, Miss Harriet?"

"But it hasn't happened yet."

"Ah! but it will—I see it all now as plain as a book. I said only last night that things were coming round nicely for us all. And they are—they are!"

Harriet began to cry, and to beg Mattie to desist. For an instant the sanguine assertion sounded like a vain prophecy, and jarred strangely on her nerves, bringing forth tears and heavy sobs, and a fear of that future which stretched forth radiantly beyond to Mattie's vision. After all, Harriet was but a girl, and had not thought very deeply of all that the contract implied between Sidney and herself. And after all, *were* things coming round nicely?—or was the red glow in the sky lurid and threatening to her, and more than her?

This is scarcely a quiet story, and we are not through our first volume. What does the astute novel-reader think?

END OF BOOK THE SECOND.

BOOK III.

UNDER SUSPICION.

CHAPTER I.

AN OLD FRIEND.

Mr. Wesden retired from business. After thirty or forty years' application to the arduous task of "keeping house and home together," after much hesitation as to whether it were safe and practicable and he could afford it; after a struggle with his old habits of shop-keeping, and a deliberate survey of his position from all points of the compass, he migrated from Great Suffolk Street, and settled down in what he considered country—a back street in the Camberwell New Road, commanding views of a cabbage-field, a public house, and another back street in course of formation by an enterprising builder.

This was country enough for Mr. Wesden; and handy for town, and Great Suffolk Street. For he had scarcely retired from business, merely withdrawn himself from the direct management, the sales over the counter, and the worry of the news-boys. The name of Wesden was still over the door, and Mattie remained general manager at the old shop, which had been her refuge from the world in the hard times of her girlhood.

Mr. and Mrs. Wesden then considered themselves in the country. They had humble notions, and a little contented them. There was a back garden with a grass plot, a gravel walk, two rows of box edging, and a few flower-beds—surely that was country enough for anybody, they thought? Then it was quite a mansion of a house—six rooms exclusive of kitchen; and, thanks more to Harriet's taste than her parents', was neatly and prettily furnished.

It was a change from Great Suffolk Street. Harriet Wesden had been brought up with lady-like notions, and had never taken to the shop; it was pleasant to live in a private house, practice her piano, assist her mother in the gardening, and have a young man to come courting her "once or twice a-week!" Mr. Wesden, with habits more formed for shop life, had to struggle hard before he could accustom himself to the novelty of his position; in his heart he never felt thoroughly at home, and was always glad of an excuse to walk over to Great Suffolk Street. He could not sit on the new chairs all day, and stare at the roses on the carpet; there was nothing much to see out of window save the postman, pot-boy, grocer's boy, and butcher, at regular intervals; gardening did not agree with his back, and it was hard work to get through the day, unless he went for a walk with the old lady.

The old lady aforesaid had taken quite a new lease of life—absence from the close neighbourhood of Suffolk Street had given her back some of her old strength; for twenty years she had solaced herself with the thought of "retiring"—the one ambition of a tradesman's wife—and now it had come, and she was all the better for the change. She made such good use of her limbs at intervals, became so absorbed in training Sweet Williams, and picking the snails off the white lilies, brightened up so much in that small suburban retreat, that the old gentleman—always be it remembered of a suspicious turn—doubted in his own mind if Mrs. W. had not been "shamming Abraham" in Great Suffolk Street.

Harriet was not nineteen years of age yet, and business had not been left in Mattie's charge three months, when Mr. Wesden's character began to mould itself afresh. The change which had done mother and daughter good, altered Mr. Wesden for the worse. He became irritable, at times a little despondent; nothing to do, began seriously to affect his temper. This is no common result in men who have been in harness all their lives—steady, energetic shopkeepers, whose lives have been one bustle for a quarter of a century and upwards, find retiring from business not so fine a thing as it looked from the distance, when they were in debt to the wholesale purveyors.

Mr. Wesden did not like it—if the truth must be spoken, though he kept it to himself, for appearances sake, he absolutely hated it. He was not intended for a gentleman, and he could *not* waste time—it made his head ache and gave him the heart-burn. If it had not been for the shop in Great Suffolk Street, he would have gone melancholy mad, or taken to drinking; that shop was his safety valve, and he was only his old self when he was back in it, pottering over the stock.

Unfortunately his *new* self was never more highly developed than when he had returned to Camberwell, and woe to the beggar or the brass band that halted before his gates and worried him.

Meanwhile, the shop in Great Suffolk Street continued to do its steady and safe business. Mattie was not far from eighteen years of age, proud of her position of trust, the quickest and best of shopkeepers. On the first floor still resided Mr. Hinchford and his son; the place was handy for office yet, and they were biding their time to launch forth, and assert their true position in society. The rent was moderate, and Sidney was trying hard to save money out of his salary; there were incentives to save, and at times he was even a trifle too economical for his father's tastes. Still, he erred on the right side—his father was becoming weaker, and his father's memory was not what it had been—his employers had not spoken of the partnership lately, and there might be rainy days ahead, which it was policy to prepare for—in a world of changes, who could tell what might happen?

Mattie found it dull at first after the Wesdens' departure; the place seemed full of echoes, and one bright face at least was hard to lose. But the face came often to light up the old shop again, and on alternate Sundays she went to dine at the fine house at Camberwell, leaving Ann Packet in charge of the establishment.

Still she was soon "at home;" she was a dependant, and must expect changes; she was a girl who always made the best of everything. There was no time for her to regret the alterations; she was born for work, and there was plenty to do in Mr. Wesden's business, not to mention a watch upon Ann Packet at times, who, when "afflicted," was rather remiss in her attentions upon the lodgers.

Life was not monotonous with her, for she took an interest in her work; and if it had been, there were many gleams of sunshine athwart it; those who knew her best, loved her and had confidence in her. Many in Suffolk Street thought there wasn't such a young woman in the world; a butcher over the way—a young man beginning business for himself, thought that it would be a "good spec" to have such a young woman behind his counter attending to the customers—those who knew her history, and there were many in Suffolk Street who remembered her antecedents, wondered at her progress; all was well until the autumn set in, and then the tide turned in the affairs of Mattie, and on those good friends whom Mattie loved.

One afternoon in September, Mattie was busy in the shop as usual—she kept to the shop all day, and never adopted the plan of hiding away from customers in the back parlour—when a woman with a large basket, a key on her little finger, a bonnet half off her head disclosing a broad, sallow, wrinkled face, came shuffling into the shop.

Mattie looked at her across the counter, and waited for orders, looked till her heart began beating unpleasantly fast. Back from the land benighted came a rush of old memories at the sight of that dirty, slip-shod woman, whom she had hoped never to see again.

"And so you recollects me, Mattie, arter all these years?"

"I—I think that I have seen you before."

"*I* should think you just had, once or twice. And so you're minding this shop for the Wesdens, whose turned gentlefolks?"

"Yes, I am."

"Well," putting her basket on the counter, and taking the one chair that was placed for the convenience of customers, "wonders will never cease. To think that you should find a place like this, and should have stuck to it so long, and never gone traipsing about the streets again."

"Can I serve you with anything?" asked Mattie.

"No, you can't. I never deal here."

"Then what do you want?"

"Ah! that's another wonder which won't cease either, my dear," said the old woman, assuming an insinuative manner, "and a bigger wonder than the tother one."

"I don't want to hear it, I don't want anything to say to you. You must go out of the shop, Mrs. Watts."

"Don't be afeard of me, my love; the Lord knows I haven't been a trouble to you, though I've lived within a stone's throw, and could have dropped in here at any moment. But no, I says, let her keep to her fine stuck up people if she likes, and forget her oldest and best friends for 'em, and do her wust, it's not the likes of me or mine who'll poke our noses into her affairs. No, I says, let her keep a lady, and wear brown meriner dresses, and smart black aprons, and white collars and cuffs, for me!"

Mrs. Watts had verged into the acrimonious vein, taken stock of Mattie's general appearance at that juncture, and introduced it into her conversation with an ease and fluency that was remarkable.

Mattie stood watching her. This was the evil genius of her early life, and there was danger in her very presence. It was not safe to take her eyes from her.

"What do you want?" she asked again.

"It's somethin' partickler—shall we come into the parler?"

"Oh! no."

"I'm not well dressed enuf, I spose?—I'm not fit society for sich a nice young gal, I spose?—I'm to be turned off as if I was a beggar, instead of the woman of property which I am, I spose?"

"What do you want?" repeated Mattie.

"And I was your poor mother's friend, and trusted her when nobody else would, and gave her a bed to die on comforbly when there wasn't a mag to be made out of her. And I was your friend, though that's something to turn your nose up at, ain't it?"

"You were kind in your way, perhaps—I cannot say, I don't know; I don't wish to remember the past any more. Will you tell me what you want, or go away?"

"And you won't come into the parler?"

"No."

"It's the curiest story as you ever did hear. There's been a man asking arter you down our court, and asking arter me, and finding me out at last, and nearly coming to a bargain with me, when, cus my greediness, I lost him."

"Asking after me?"

"Ah! you may well open those black eyes of yourn—he made me stare, I can tell you. He walks one day into my house, as if it belonged to him, and says, 'Are you Mrs. Watts?' 'Yes,' I says. 'Do you remember Mrs. Gray?' he says. 'Not by name,' I says. 'She was a tramp,' he says, 'and died here.' 'Oh!' I says, 'if it's her you mean, whose name I never knowed or cared about, died here, she did.' 'And the child?' he says. 'Mattie you mean,' I says. 'Ah! Mattie,' he says. And then I says, thinking it was a dodge, my dear, for the perlice are up to all manner of tricks, and you mightn't have been going on the square, and been wanted, then I says, 'And will you obleege me with your reasons for all these questions of a 'spectable and hard-working woman?' I says. 'My name's Gray,' he says, 'and I'm Mattie's father.'"

"Is this true?—oh! is it really true?"

"Hopemaydropdead, my dear, if it isn't," Mrs. Watts remarked, running her words into each other in the volubility of her protestation; "hopemayneverstiragainfromhere, if t'isn't, *Miss Gray*! 'Mattie's father,' I says. 'Yes,' he says; 'is that so very wonderful?' And I says, 'Yes it is, arter all this time ago.' And then he asks all manner of questions, which I didn't see the good of answering, and so was werry ignorant, my dear, until he said he'd give me a suverin to find you out. I says, 'I'd try for a five pun note, for you was a long way off, and it'd be a trouble to look arter you.' And he says, 'I'll take that trouble,' and I didn't see the pull of that, knowing he was anxious like, and fancying that five pounds wouldn't ruin him, so I held out. And then he looked at his watch, and said he'd come again, which he never did, as I'm an honest ooman."

"How long was this ago?"

"Two months."

"What kind of a man was he?"

"Oh! a little ugly bloke enough—not too well dressed. Your father won't turn out to be a duke or markis, if he ever turns up agin and brings me my five pounds."

"But you will not tell him where I live?—he may be a bad, cruel man—my mother ran away from him because he treated her ill, I have heard her say. Oh! don't tell him where I live—I am happy and contented here."

Mrs. Watts brightened up with a new idea. "You must make it a five pun note, then, instead of him, and I'll tell him I can't find yer when he comes back to take you home with him. You've saved money, I daresay, by this time, and five pounds ain't much to stand."

Mattie recovered her composure when it came to the money test; there was a motive for Mrs. Watts' appearance there, she thought; after all it was an idle story, a foolish scheme to extort money, which Mattie saw through now.

"I shall not give you any money—not five pence, Mrs. Watts."

"Leave it alone, then," was the sharp reply; "you can't leave here, and I'll bring him to you, if he ever comes agin. I didn't come to get money out of yer, but to keep my eye upon you for your father's sake. And you'll never take a step away from this place, right or left, but what I'll know it—there's too many on us about here for you to steal away."

"I do not intend to steal away," cried Mattie.

"And considerin' that I've come out of kindness, and to give you a piece of news, you might have said thankee for it—bad luck to you, Mattie Gray."

"Oh! bad luck will not come to me at your wish."

The old woman paused at the door, and shook her key at her.

"I never wished bad luck to any living soul, but what it came. Now think of that!"

She went out of the shop and along Great Suffolk Street at a smart pace—like a woman who had suddenly remembered something and started off in a hurry after it. Mattie was perplexed at the interview; doubtful if any truth had mixed itself with Mrs. Watts' statement, and at a loss to reconcile all that she had heard with fabrication. Even from Mrs. Watts' lips it sounded like truth; the woman seemed in earnest, her offer to take five pounds for her silence an impromptu thought, originated by Mattie's sudden fear.

"What can it mean?—what can it mean?" reiterated Mattie to herself; "was it unfair to doubt her?—she thought so, or she would not have wished me bad luck so evilly at the last?"

She sat down behind the counter to reflect upon the strangeness of the incident, and was still revolving in her mind the facts or falsities connected with it, when Ann Packet burst from the parlour door into the shop, with eyes distended.

"Have you been up-stairs, Mattie?"

"Upstairs, Ann!—no."

"Have you been asleep?"

"No."

"Oh, lor!—quite sure—not a moment!"

"No—no—what has happened!"

"Somebody's been up-stairs into all the rooms, into yourn, too, where the money's put for Mr. Wesden—and—and broken open the drawer."

"And the cash box that I keep there?"

"Open, and EMPTY!"

Mattie dropped again into the chair from which she had risen at the appearance of Ann Packet, and struggled with a sense of faintness which came over her. The bad luck that Mrs. Watts had wished had soon stolen on its way towards her.

CHAPTER II.

STRANGE VISITORS TO GREAT SUFFOLK STREET.

Mattie guessed the plan by which the robbery had been effected, and at which Mrs. Watts had connived. Her attention had been distracted by the story that had been fabricated for the purpose, and then the accomplice, on his hands and knees, had stolen snake-like towards the door opening on the stairs, and made short work with everything of value to be found in the upper floors. What was to be done?—what would Mr. Wesden say, he who had never had a robbery committed on his premises during all the long years of his business life, thanks to his carefulness and watchfulness? What would he think of her? Would he believe that she had paid common attention to the shop he had left in trust to her, to be robbed in the broad noonday? What should she do? wait till the shop was closed and then set forth for Camberwell with the bad news, or start at once, leaving Ann Packet in charge, or wait till Mr. Hinchford came home, and ask him to be the mediator?

Whilst revolving these plans of action in her mind, the proprietor of the establishment, wearied of his country retirement, walked into the shop.

"Oh! sir, something has happened very dreadful!" she exclaimed.

Mr. Wesden began to stare over her head at this salutation.

"What's that?" he asked.

"Some one has been up-stairs this afternoon, broken open the drawers, and the cash-box, and taken the money, eight pounds, nine shillings and sixpence, sir."

Mr. Wesden sat down in the chair formerly occupied by Mrs. Watts and tried to arrange his ideas; he stared over Mattie's head harder than ever; he held his own head between his hands, taking off his hat especially for that purpose, and placing it on the counter.

"Money taken out of *this* house?"

"Yes."

"At *this* time of day—where were you, Mattie?"

"In the shop, sitting here, I believe."

"Then they came in at the back, I suppose?"

"No, in the front, whilst Mrs. Watts was talking to me."

"What Mrs. Watts?—not the woman——"

"Yes, yes, the woman who would have tempted me to evil, years ago; she came into the shop this afternoon, and said that my father—as if I'd ever had one, sir!—had been inquiring for me in Kent Street."

"This is a curious story," muttered Mr. Wesden.

He put on his hat and went up-stairs; it was half an hour, or an hour before he reappeared, looking very grave and stern.

"They didn't come in at the back of the house—I can't make it out—eight pounds nine and sixpence is a heavy loss—I'll speak to the policeman."

Mr. Wesden went in search of a policeman, and presently returned with two members of the official force, with whom he went up-stairs, and with whom he remained some time. After a while Mr. Hinchford, senior, came home, heard the tidings, went into his room, and discovered a little money missing also, besides a watch-chain which he had left at home that day for security's sake, a link having snapped, and repairs being necessary.

Mr. Wesden and the policemen came down stairs and put many questions to Mattie and Ann Packet; finally the policemen departed, and Mr. Wesden very gravely walked about the shop, and paid but little attention to Mattie's expressions of regret.

"It's my carelessness, sir, and I hope you'll let me make it up. I've been saving money, sir, lately, thanks to you."

"Well, you can't say fairer than that, Mattie," he responded to this suggestion; "I'll think about that, and let you know to-morrow."

He never let Mattie know his determination, or seemed inclined to dwell upon the subject again; the robbery became a forbidden topic, and drifted slowly away from the present. But it was an event that saddened Mattie; for she could read that Mr. Wesden had formed his own ideas of its occurrence, and she tortured herself with the fear that he might suspect her. She had gained his confidence only to lose it; her antecedents were dark enough, and if he did not believe all that she had told him, then he must doubt if she were the proper person to manage the place in his absence.

He said nothing; he suggested no alteration; but he came more frequently to business; and he *was* altered in his manner towards her.

Mattie was right—he suspected her; he thought he kept his suspicions to himself, for amidst the new distrust rose ever before him the past struggles of the girl in her faithful service to him, and he was not an uncharitable man. But the police had seconded his doubts—the story was an unlikely one, Mattie had been a bad character, and, above all, Mrs. Watts, upon inquiry, had not lived in Kent Street or parts adjacent for the last three years.

However, his better nature would not misjudge implicitly, although a shadow of distrust was between him and Mattie from that day forth. He said nothing to Harriet or his wife, but he seldom asked Mattie to his house at Camberwell now; he came more frequently for his money, and looked more closely after his stock; he had a habit of turning into the shop at unseasonable hours and taking her by surprise there.

Mattie bore with this for a while—for two or three months, perhaps, then her out-spoken nature faced Mr. Wesden one evening.

"You've got a bad thought in your head against me, sir."

Thus taxed, Mr. Wesden answered in the negative. Looking at her fearless face, and her bright eyes that so steadily met his, he had not the heart or the courage to confess it.

"I'd rather go away than you should think that; go away and leave you all for ever. I know," she added, very sorrowfully and humbly, "that my past life isn't a fair prospect to look back upon, and that it stands between you and your trust in me at this time."

"No, Mattie."

"If you doubt me——"

"If I believed that you were not acting fairly by me, I should not have you here an hour," he said.

He was carried away by Mattie's earnestness; he forgot his new harshness, which he had inherited with his change of life; before him stood the girl who had nursed his wife through a long illness, and he could not believe in her ingratitude towards him. After that charge and refutation, Mattie and Mr. Wesden were on better terms with each other—the robbery, the visit of Mrs. Watts, appeared all parts of a bad dream, difficult to shake off, but in the reality of which it was hard to believe. And yet it was all a terrible truth, too, and the story, true or false, of Mrs. Watts, late of Kent Street, had left its impression on Mattie, deep and ineffaceable; she could almost believe that from the shadowy past some stranger, cruel and villainous, would step forth to claim her.

Meantime the course of Sidney Hinchford's true love flowed on peacefully; he was happy enough now—with the hope of Harriet Wesden for a wife he became more energetic than ever in business; possibly even a young man less abrupt to his companions in office; for the tender passion softens the heart wonderfully. He was more kind and less brusque in his manner. To Mattie he had been always kind, but she fancied that even she could detect a different and more gentle way with him.

When he returned from Camberwell—Mr. Wesden always shut him out at early hours—he generally brought some message from Harriet to the old half-friend and confidante, and at times would loiter about the shop talking of Harriet to Mattie, and sure of her sympathy with all that he said and did.

On one of the latter occasions, about six in the evening, he remarked,

"When Harriet and I are grand enough to have a large house of our own—for we can't tell what may happen—I shall ask you to be our housekeeper, Mattie."

Mattie's face brightened up; it had been rather a sad face of late, and Sidney Hinchford had observed it, and been puzzled at the reason. The story of the robbery had not affected him much.

"Oh! then I'll pray night and day for the big house, Mr. Sidney," she said, with her usual readiness of reply.

"Why, Mattie, are you tired of shop-keeping?"

"At times I am," she answered. "I don't know why. I don't see how to get on and feel happy. It's rather lonely here."

"You dissatisfied, Mattie! Why, I have always regarded you as the very picture of content."

"I'm not dissatisfied exactly; don't tell any one that, or they'll think I'm ungrateful for all the kindness that has been shown me, and all the confidence that has been placed in me. You, Mr. Hinchford, must not think I'm ungrateful or discontented."

"Perhaps you're ambitious, Mattie," he said, jestingly, "now you've mastered all the lessons which I used to set you, and can read and write as well as most of us."

"I don't exactly understand the true meaning of ambition," said Mattie. "I'm no scholar, you know. Is it a wish to get on in the world?"

"Partly."

"I'm not ambitious. I wouldn't be a lady for the world. I would rather be of service to someone I love, than see those I love working and toiling for my sake. But then they must love me, and have faith in me, or I'm—I'm done for!"

Mattie had dropped, as was her habit when excited, into one of her old phrases; but its meaning was apparent, and Sidney Hinchford understood it.

"Something's on your mind, Mattie. Can I punch anybody's head for you?"

"No, thank you. But you can remember the promise about the housekeeper when you're a rich man."

Like Sidney's father, she accepted Sidney's coming greatness as a thing of course, concerning which no doubts need be entertained.

He laughed.

"It's a promise, mind. Good night, Mattie."

"Good night."

That night was to be marked by another variation of the day's monotony—by more than one. It was striking seven from St. George's Church, Southwark, when a stately carriage and pair dashed up Great Suffolk Street, and drew up at the stationer's door. A few moments afterwards a tall, white-haired old gentleman entered the shop leaning upon the arm of a good-looking young man, and advanced towards the counter.

The likeness of the elder man was so apparent to that of old Mr. Hinchford up-stairs, that Mattie fancied it was he for an instant, until her rapid observation detected that the gentleman before her was much thinner, wore higher shirt collars, had a voluminous frill to his shirt, and a double gold eye-glass in his hand.

"Thank you, that will do. I won't trouble you any further."

"Shall I wait here?"

"No, my boy—don't let me keep you from your club engagements. If you are behind time take the carriage."

"No, no—not so selfish as that, sir. Good night."

"Good night."

The good-looking young man did not wait to see the result of his father's mission; he glanced for a moment at Mattie, and then took his departure, leaving the stately old gentleman confronting her at the counter.

"This is Mr. Wesden's, stationer, I believe?" he asked, surveying Mattie through his glasses.

"Yes, sir."

"A Mr. Hinchford lives here?"

"Yes, sir."

"Is he within?"

"Not the old gentleman, I believe, sir."

"As I have not come hither to base my hopes of an interview on the belief of a black-eyed shop-girl, will you be kind enough to inquire?"

The old gentleman sat down and loosened the gilt clasp of a long cloak which he wore—an old-fashioned, oddly cut black cloak, with a cape to it.

Mattie forgot the likeness which this gentleman bore to the lodger up-stairs; lost her impression of the carriage at the door, and thought of Mrs. Watts and the hundred tricks of London thieves. She began thumping with her heels on the floor, until she quite shook up the old gentleman on the other side of the counter.

"What's that for, my child?" he asked.

"That'll bring up the servant—I never leave the shop."

The gentleman closed his glasses, and rapped upon the counter with them, in rather an amused manner.

"By Jupiter Tonans, that's amusing! She thinks I am going to make off with the stationery," he said, more to himself than Mattie.

Ann Packet, round eyed and wondering as usual, looked over the parlour blind. Mattie beckoned to her, and she opened the parlour door.

"Run up and tell Mr. Sidney that a gentleman wishes to see his father. Is he to wait, or to call again?"

"I think I might answer that question better myself—stay."

The slim old gentleman very slowly and deliberately searched for his card-case, produced it and drew forth a card.

"Present that to Mr. Sidney, and say that the bearer is desirous of an interview."

Ann Packet took the card in her great red hand, turned it over, looked from it to the owner, gave vent to an idiotic "Lor!" and then trudged up-stairs with the card. Mattie and the old gentleman, meanwhile, continued to regard each other—the suspicions of the former not perfectly allayed yet.

Ann Packet returned, appearing by the staircase door this time.

"Mr. Sidney Hinchford will see you, sir—if your business is of importance, he says."

The gentleman addressed compressed his lips—very thin lips they became on the instant—but deigned no reply. He rose from his chair, and followed Ann through the door, up-stairs towards Mr. Hinchford's room, leaving his hat on the counter, where he had very politely placed it upon entering the shop.

Mattie put it behind her, and then scowled down a lack-a-daisical footman, who was simpering at her between a *Family Herald* and a portrait of T. P. Cooke.

The stranger followed Ann Packet up-stairs, and entered the room on the first floor, glancing sharply round him through his glasses, and taking a survey of everything which it contained on the instant. There was a fire burning in the grate that autumn night; the gas was lighted; the tea-things ready on the table; at a smaller table by the window, working by the light of a table-lamp adorned with a green shade, and with another green shade tied across his forehead by way of extra protection for the eyes he worked so mercilessly, sat Sidney Hinchford, the only occupant of the room.

Sidney rose, bowed slightly, pointed to a chair with the feather of his pen, then sat down again, and looked at his visitor from under the ugly shade, which cast his face into shadow.

The gentleman bowed also, and took the seat indicated, keeping his gold-rimmed glasses on his nose.

"You are my brother James's son, I presume?"

"The same, sir."

"You are surprised to see me here?"

"Yes, sir—now."

"Why now?" was the quick question that followed like the snap of a trigger.

"Years and years ago, when I was a lad, I fancied that you might visit here, and make an effort to bridge over an ugly gulf, sir."

"Years and years ago, young man, I had too much upon my mind, and, it was just possible, more pride in my heart than to make the first advances."

"You were the richer man—and you had done the wrong."

"Wrong, sir!" replied the other; "there was no wrong done that I am aware of. I was a man careful of my money, and your father was a man improvident with his. Was it wrong to object to an alliance?"

"I have but a dim knowledge of the story, sir. My father does not care to dwell upon it."

"I will tell it you."

The old gentleman drew his chair nearer to Sidney; the young man held up his hand.

"Pardon me, but I have no desire to hear it. Were I to press my father, I could learn it from his own lips. Please state the object of your coming hither."

"To make the first advances in the latter days that have come to him and me," he said; "can I say more? To help him if he be in distress—and to assist his son if he find the world hard to cope with. It is a romantic appearance, a romantic penitence if you will, for not allowing your father to spend my money as well as his own," he added, with a slight curl of the lip, which turned Sidney suddenly against him; "but it is an effort to bridge over the gulf to which you have recently alluded."

"I fear my father will not thank you for the effort," was the cold reply; "and for the help which you would offer now, I can answer for his refusal."

"Ah! he was always a proud fellow, and blind to his own interest," was the quiet observation here; "his friends laughed at his pride, and traded in his weakness before you were born."

"He has one friend living who respects them now, sir."

"His son, I presume?"

"His son, sir."

"I am glad that his son is so high-spirited; but he will find that amiable feeling rather in the way of his advancement."

"No, sir—I think not."

Mr. Hinchford regarded Sidney very closely; he did not appear put out by the young man's retorts, and he was pleased at the effect that his own satire had upon him.

"Well," he said at last, "I have not come to quarrel with my nephew—I am here as a peace-maker, and, lo! the son starts up with all the father's old obstinacies. Your name is Sidney, I believe."

"Yes, sir."

"Sidney Hinchford, then," said he, "if you be a man of the world—which I fancy you are—you will not turn your back on your own interests for the sake of the grudge which my unforgiving brother may owe me. That's not the way of the world, unless it's the world of silly novel-writers and poets."

"Sir, this sudden interest in my father and myself is somewhat unaccountable."

"Granted," was the cool response.

"Still, let me for my father and myself thank you," said Sidney, with a graceful dignity that set well upon him, "thank you for this sudden offer, which I, for both, must unhesitatingly decline."

"Indeed!"

"We are not rich, you can see," Sidney said with a comprehensive sweep of his hand, "but we have managed to exist without getting into debt, and I believe that the worst struggle is over with us both."

"Upon what supposition do you base this theory?"

"No matter, Mr. Hinchford, my belief is strong, and I would not deprive myself of the pleasure of saying that I worked on with my father to the higher ground without the help of those rich relations who would at the eleventh hour have taken the credit to themselves."

"You are a remarkable young man."

"Sir, you come too late here," said Sidney, with no small amount of energy; "we bear you no ill-will, but we will not have your help now. If you and yours forgot my father in his adversity, if you made no sign when he was troubled by my mother's death, if you held aloof when assistance and sympathy would have made amends for the old breach between you, if you turned your backs upon him and shut him from your thoughts then, now we repudiate your service, and prefer to work our way alone!"

"Well, well, be it so," said his uncle; "it is heroic, but it is bad policy, more especially in you, a young man who will have to fight hard for a competence. You will excuse this whim of mine."

"I have already thanked you for the good intention."

"I did not anticipate encountering so hard and dogmatic a disposition as your own, but I do not regret the visit."

Sidney looked at his watch, fidgeted with the feather of his pen, but made no remark to this.

"We will say it was a whim—you will please to inform your father that this was simply a whim of mine—the impulse of a moment, after an extra glass of port wine with my dessert."

"I will think so, if you wish it."

"You perceive that I am an old man—your father's senior by eight years—and old people *do* get whimsical and childish, when the iron in their nerves melts, by some unaccountable process, away from them. Possibly this is not the first time that it has struck me that my brother James and I might easily arrive at a better appreciation of each other's character, if we sat down quietly face to face, two old men as we have become. The sarcasm that wounded him, and the passionate impulse that irritated me, would have grown less with our white hairs, I think. I don't know for certain—I cannot answer for a man who always would take the wrong side of an argument, and stick to it. By Gad! how tightly he would stick to it!"

The old gentleman rapped his gold-headed cane on the floor, and indulged in a little sharp laugh, not unpleasant to hear. Sidney repressed a smile, and looked significantly at his watch again.

"You wish me gone, young sir," said his uncle.

"Candidly, I see no good result to arise from your stay. My father is of an excitable disposition, and, I am sorry to say, neither so strong nor so well as I could wish. I fear the shock would be too much for him."

"I will take the hint," he said, rising; "I hate scenes, and if there is likely to be a second edition of those covert reproaches with which you have favoured me, why, it is best to withdraw as gracefully as possible, under the circumstances. You will tell him that I have called?"

"Yes, sir."

"You will tell him also—bear this in mind instead of sucking your pen, will you?—that if he owe me no ill-will, he will call on me next—that it is *his* turn! I never ask a man twice for anything—except for the money he may owe me," he added, drily.

"I will deliver your message, Mr. Hinchford."

"Then I have the honour, sir, to apologize for this intrusion, and to wish you a good evening."

He crossed the room and held out a thin white hand to Sidney, looking very strangely, very intently at him meanwhile. Sidney placed his own within it, almost instinctively, and the two Hinchfords shook hands.

They parted; Sidney thought that he had finally taken his departure, when the door opened, and he reappeared.

"Do you mind showing me a light?—it's a corkscrew staircase, leading to the bottomless pit, to all appearances."

Sidney seized the table-lamp, and proceeded to the top of the stairs, which his uncle descended in a slow and gingerly manner. At the first landing he looked up, and said:

"That will do, thank you—remember, *his* turn next—good evening."

Sidney went back to the room, and shortly afterwards Mr. Hinchford, the great banker, the owner of princely estates in three counties, was whirled away westward in his carriage.

CHAPTER III.

SIDNEY'S SUGGESTION.

When Mr. Hinchford returned home, Sidney related the particulars of the strange visit that he had received; and from the effect which the news produced on his father, was grateful for the thought which had prompted him to request his uncle's departure. Sidney had noticed with sadness, lately, that his father was easily disturbed, easily affected, and it was satisfactory to know that it had been judicious on his part to advise his uncle's retirement.

Mr. Hinchford tugged at his stock, held his temples, passed his hands through his scanty hair, puffed and blowed, dropped his first cup of tea over his knees, and did not subside into a moderate state of calmness for at least a quarter of an hour after the story had been told.

"And so brother Geoffry turns up at last!—well, I thought he would."

Sidney looked with amazement at his father.

"He would have turned up years ago, I daresay, if it hadn't been for his wife—she and I never agreed; but old steady, quiet Geoffry, why, when we were boys, we were the best of friends."

"You certainly surprise me, father. Perhaps I have done wrong in persuading him to depart. But I always understood that it had been a desperate quarrel between you, and that you had almost taken an oath never to speak to him again."

"That's all true enough, and it was a desperate quarrel, and he was tight-fisted just then, and let me drift into bankruptcy, rather than help me. It wasn't brotherly, and I'll never forgive him—never. How was the rascal looking, Sid?"

"Like a spare likeness of yourself, sir."

"He's taller than I am by a good two inches. We used to cut notches in the sides of all the doors, when we were boys; comparing notes, we called it. I suppose he's very much altered?"

"Well, never having seen him before, it is difficult to say. But I have no doubt that there's a difference in him since you met last."

"Let me see—it's five-and-twenty years ago, come next February. Twenty-five years to nurse a quarrel, and bear enmity in one's heart against him. What a time!"

"He was anxious to tell me the story of that quarrel, sir, but I declined to listen to it."

"I hope you weren't rude."

"Oh! no, sir."

"You have a most unpleasant habit of blurting out anything that comes uppermost. That's your great failing, Sid."

"I like to speak out, sir."

"And after all, perhaps if we had spoken out less—he and I—we should not have been all these years at arm's length, and you might have been the better for that. There's no telling, things turn out so strangely. And it wasn't so much his refusal to lend me, his only brother, ten thousand pounds—ten drops of water to him—but the way in which he refused, the bitterness of his words, the gall and wormwood instead of brotherly sympathy. I was half mad with my losses, and he stung me with his cool and insolent taunts, and cast me off to beggary—Sid, would you forgive that?"

Mr. Hinchford had realized the scene again; through the mists of five-and-twenty years, it shone forth vividly; his cheek flushed, and his hand smote the table heavily, and made the tea things jump again.

Sidney cooled him by a few words.

"He has been cautious with his money, and you might have shown signs of being reckless with yours, at that time. Possibly you both were heated, and said more than you intended. It don't appear to me to have been a very serious affair, after all."

"Did he ever seek me out again, or care whether I was alive or dead, until to-day?—was that kind?"

"Did you ever seek *him* out!"

"He was the rich man, and I the poor, Sid."

"Ah! that makes a difference!"

"What would you have done?" he asked anxiously.

"Kept away; not because it was right or politic, but because I inherit my father's pride."

"It's an odd legacy, Sid," remarked the father, mournfully.

"I told him to-night we did not care about his patronage, and could work our way in the world—that at so late an hour, when the worst was over, we would prefer to thank ourselves for the result. I don't say that I was right, father," he added; "but there was a satisfaction in saying so, and in showing that we did not jump at any favour he might think it friendly to concede."

"You're a brave lad," remarked the father, relapsing into thought again; "and perhaps it is as well to show we don't care for him. He talked about my turn next, you say?"

"Yes."

"That means, that he'll never come here again, or make another effort to be friends. Oh! he's as hard as iron when he says a thing, Sid."

"Shall I tell you what I have thought, sir?—it goes against the foolish oath you took, but I think you'll be forgiven for it."

"What have you thought?" he asked with eagerness.

"That it shall be our turn some day—some early day, I hope—to visit him, and say:—'We are in a good position in life, and above all help, shall we be friends again?'"

"To walk into his counting-house, and surprise him?" cried the father; "for me to say:—'I owe all to my son's energy and cleverness, and can afford to face you, without being suspected of wanting your money.' Well, we ought to bear and forbear; I don't think it would be so very hard to make it up with him!"

It was a subject that discomposed Mr. Hinchford—that kept him restless and disturbed. His son detected this, and brushed all the papers into a heap, thrust them into the recesses of his desk, and began hunting about for the backgammon-board. The past had been ever a subject kept in the background, and of late years his father had not seemed capable of hearing any news, good or bad, with a fair semblance of composure. The change in him had been a matter of regret with Sidney; far off in the distance, perhaps, there might loom a great trouble for him—he almost fancied so at times. Meanwhile, there were troubles nearer than that fancied one—man is born unto them, as the sparks fly upwards.

CHAPTER IV.

PERPLEXITY.

Harriet Wesden had spoken more than once to Mattie of the Eveleighs, a family which plays no part in these pages, although, from Harriet's knowledge of it, every after page of this story will be influenced. A Miss Eveleigh, an only daughter, and a spoiled one, had been a schoolfellow of Harriet's; an intimacy had existed between them in the old days, and when school days were ended for good, a correspondence was kept up, which resulted, eventually, in flying visits to each other's houses—the house in Camberwell, and Miss Eveleigh's residence at New Cross.

Harriet, during the last week or two, had been spending her time at New Cross with the Eveleighs, much to the desolateness of the Camberwell domicile, and the dulness of Master Sidney Hinchford. But the visit was at an end on the morning of the day alluded to in our last chapter, and had it not been for his father's excitability, Sidney, who had mapped his plans out, would have abandoned the backgammon board and a-wooing gone.

It was as well that he did not, for Harriet Wesden at half-past seven in the evening entered the stationer's shop, and surprised Mattie by her late visit.

"Good gracious!" was Mattie's truly feminine ejaculation, "who would have thought of seeing you to-night? How well you are looking—how glad I am that you have come back—what a colour you have got!"

"Have I?" she said; "ah! it's the sharp frost that's in the streets to-night. Let me deliver father's message, and hurry back before he gets fidgety about me."

Harriet Wesden and Mattie went into the parlour, Mattie taking up her position by the door, so as to command the approach from the street, Harriet sitting by the fire with her head against the chimney-piece. The message was delivered, sundry little account books were wanted at once, and Harriet was to take them back with her; Mattie had to find them in the shop, and make them up into a little parcel for our heroine.

When she returned, Harriet was in the same position, staring very intently at the fire.

"Is anything the matter?" asked our heroine.

"Oh! no—what should be the matter, dear?"

"You're very thoughtful, and it's not exactly your look, Miss Harriet."

"Fancies again, Mattie," remarked Harriet; "I'm only a little tired, having walked from Camberwell."

"I hope you'll not walk back—it's getting late. Unless," she added, archly, "Mr. Sidney up-stairs is to see you safely home. That must be one of the nicest parts of courtship, to go arm-in-arm together about the streets—to feel yourself safe with *him* at your side."

Harriet's thoughtful demeanour vanished; she gave a merry laugh at the gravity with which Mattie delivered this statement, taunted Mattie with having thoughts of a lover running in her head, darted from that subject to the pleasant fortnight she had been spending with the Eveleighs at New Cross, detailed the particulars of her visit, the people to whom she had been introduced, and lively little incidents connected with them—finally caught up her parcel and bade Mattie good night.

"Ah! you'll wait till I call down Mr. Sidney, I'm sure."

"He'll think that I have called for him. No, I'm going home alone to-night."

"Why, what will he say?"

"Tell him that I was in a hurry, going home by omnibus to save time, and appease father's nervousness about me. I will not have any danglers in my train to-night. I'm in a bad temper—nervous, irritable and excitable—I shall only offend him."

"Then something has——"

"Good night, Mattie—oh! I had nearly forgotten to ask you to dine with us on Sunday; you'll be sure to come early?"

"Who told you to say that?"

"Why, my father, to be sure."

"I'm glad of it—I'm glad he thinks better of me," Mattie cried; "oh! Miss Harriet, you don't know how miserable I have been in my heart, lest he—lest he has thought differently of me lately!"

"More fancies! I have always said that they were fancies, Mattie."

"Ah! I guess pretty near to the truth sometimes."

"And tease yourself with a false idea more often—why, you will imagine that *I* shall think differently of you presently."

"No—I don't think you will."

"Never, Mattie."

"God bless you for that!—if ever I'm in trouble I shall look to you to defend me."

"And in my trouble, Mattie?" was the half-laughing rejoinder.

"I'll think of you only, fight for you against all your enemies—die for you, if it will do any good. Oh! Miss Harriet, you are growing up a lady very far above me, getting out of my reach like, you won't forget the little girl you were kind to, and shut her wholly from your heart?"

Harriet Wesden was touched; ever a sensitive girl, the sight of another's sorrow struck home. She went back a step or two into the parlour.

"This isn't like the old Mattie," she said, "the Mattie who always looked at the brightest side of life, and made the best of every difficulty. Is that silly affair of the robbery still preying on your mind?"

"On your father's perhaps—not on mine."

"Then I'll fight the battle for you to begin with—if there be really one doubt in my father's heart, I'll charge it from its hiding-place to-night. Perhaps I have been wrapped up too much lately in my own selfish thoughts when I might have helped you, Mattie. Will you forgive me?"

She stooped and kissed Mattie, whose arms closed round her for a minute with a loving clasp.

"I'm better now," said Mattie, "it was fancy, perhaps, a fancy that you, too, were going further away from me—perhaps thinking ill of me. For you were cold and distant when you came here first to-night."

"No, no."

"Well, that was my fancy, too, it's very likely. I'll say good night now, for it's getting late."

"Good night, then."

At the door she paused and returned.

"Mattie, put on your bonnet and come with me to the end of the street where the omnibus passes. I'm nervous to-night—I don't care to walk alone about these streets again."

"Let me call Mr. Sid——"

"No, no; you—not him!" she interrupted.

"I never leave the shop, Miss Harriet; it's my trust, and your father would not like it. Shall Ann——"

"Oh! it does not matter much; you have only made me nervous. I'm very wrong to seek to take you from the business, and father so particular and fidgety. I daresay no one will fly away with me. Good night, my dear."

She went away with a bright smile at her own nervousness. That was the last gleam of brightness there for awhile!

After that there settled on her face a confused expression, often a sad, always a thoughtful one, with a long look ahead, as it were from the depths of her blue eyes. From that night there was a change in her; Mattie, quick of observation, was the first to detect it. It was a face of trouble, and Mattie, seeing it now and then, could note the shadows deepen. Sidney observed it next, detected with a lover's jealous scrutiny a difference in her manner towards him, a something new which was colder and less friendly, and yet not demonstrative enough for him to murmur against, even if his half engagement had permitted him.

He asked her once if he had offended her, and she replied in the negative, and was kinder towards him for that night; but the reserve, indifference, coldness, or whatever it was, came back, and perplexed Sidney Hinchford more than he cared to own. The year of his novitiate was approaching to an end, and he thought that he could afford to wait till then; she was not tiring of him and his attentions, he had too good an opinion of himself to believe that; at times he solaced himself with the idea that she was reflecting on the gravity of the next step, that formal engagement to be married in the future to him.

Mattie and Sidney were both observers of some power, for after all they saw through the bright side—the forced side—of her. For the father and mother was reserved Harriet Wesden with her mask off.

Fathers and mothers are strangely blind to the causes of their daughters' ailments—this humble pair formed no exception to the rule. They were perplexed with her fits of brooding, her forced efforts to rally when taxed with them, her pallor, loss of appetite, red eyes and restless looks in the morning. Mr. Wesden, a suspicious man to the world in general, was the most trustful and simple as regarded his daughter; he did not know the depth of his love for her until she began to look ill, and then he almost worried her into a real illness by his suggestions and anxiety.

Mr. and Mrs. Wesden had many secret confabulations concerning the change in Harriet; pottering over a hundred fusty ideas, with never a thought as to the true one.

Was Camberwell disagreeing with her?—was the house damp, or her room badly situated?—had not the dear girl change enough, society enough?—what *was* the matter? Mr. Wesden set it down for "a low way"—an unaccountable complaint from which people suffer at times, and for which change of scene is good.

So he set to work studying the matter, originating small excursions for the day, submitting her to the healthy excitement of the winter course of lectures at the infant schools in the vicinity—lectures on artificial memory, on hydrostatics with experiments, on the poets with experiments also, and unaccountable ones they were—even once ventured into a box of the Surrey Theatre, and began to flatter himself and wife that at last Harriet was rapidly improving.

But Harriet Wesden was only learning rapidly to disguise that "something" which was perplexing her more and more with every day; learning to subdue her parents' anxiety, and sinking a little deeper all the new thoughts. But the whirl of events brought the secret uppermost, and betrayed her—she was forced to make a confidante, and she thought of Mattie, who had always loved her, and stood her friend—Mattie, in whom she was sure was the only one she could trust.

The confidence was placed suddenly, and at a time when Mattie was scarcely prepared for it—Mattie who yet, by some strange instinct, had been patiently waiting for it.

"I believe when that girl's in trouble, she will come to me," Mattie thought, "for she knows I would do anything to serve her. Have I any one to love except her in the world?—is there any one who requires so much love to keep her, what I call, strong?"

Mattie had seen that Harriet Wesden was not strong—that she was tender-hearted, affectionate, and weak—that there were times when she might give way without a strong heart and a stout hand to assist her. She had been a weak, impulsive, passionate child—she had grown up a woman very different to Mattie, whose firmness, and even hardness, had made Harriet wonder more than once. And Mattie had often wondered at Harriet in her turn—at her vanity and romantic ideas, and made excuses for her, as we all do, for those we love very dearly. She had even feared for her, until the half engagement with Sidney Hinchford had taken place, and then she had noticed that Harriet had become more staid and womanly, and was glad in her heart that it had happened thus.

Then finally and suddenly the last change swept over the surface of things—all the worse for our characters perhaps, but infinitely better for our story, which takes a new lease of life from this page.

CHAPTER V.

MR. WESDEN TURNS ECCENTRIC.

The nights "drew in" more and more; and nearer and nearer with the shortest day approached the end of Sidney Hinchford's probation. Only a week or two between the final explanations of Sid's position—of his chances in the future perhaps—everything very quiet and still at Suffolk Street and Camberwell—a deceptive calm before the storm that was brewing.

Harriet Wesden called more frequently at the stationer's shop; she was glad to escape from the long evenings at home, and the watchful, ever anxious eyes of her father, and it was easy to frame an excuse to repair to Great Suffolk Street. Occasionally Sidney Hinchford knew of her propinquity, and escorted her home—more often missed his chances of a *tête-à-tête*—three or four times, and greatly to his annoyance, crossed her in the journey, and reached Camberwell to spend the evening with a fidgety old man and his invalid spouse.

At this time it also happened that Sidney Hinchford fell into a dreamy absent way, for which there appeared no valid reasons, unless he had become alive to the doubts of Harriet's affection for him; an absence of mind, and even an irritability, which was disguised well enough from the father—before whom Sidney was more or less an actor—but which Mattie, ever on the watch, was quick as usual to detect.

She had become puzzled by Harriet's abstraction, and had looked for its reflex at once in Sidney Hinchford's face—finding it there, as she thought, after a while.

Mattie, left in the dark as to the truth, and every day becoming more of a young woman, who knew her place, and felt the distance between her master's daughter, her master's lodgers, and herself, could but draw her own conclusions, and frame a story from them.

Harriet and Sidney had quarrelled, and were keeping their quarrel a secret from the good folk at Camberwell; something had happened to cast a gloom on the way that Mattie thought would be ever bright and rosy, and each day they who should have been lovers seemed drifting further apart. She would have liked to play the part of mediator between them—to see them friends again—but her position held her back, and she had not the courage of a year ago. Those two young lovers had been the bright figures in her past—her life had somehow become blended with them, and she felt that her interest was of a cumulative character, and not likely to die out with her riper womanhood. She could not disassociate her mind away from them; at every turn in her career they were before her—they haunted her thoughts, and harassed her with their seeming inconsistencies of conduct. She did not understand them, for the clue to the inner life was absent from her; she could not see why Harriet was not a girl to love this young man with all her heart, as she was loved—she felt that there was an assimilation between the strength of one, and the weakness that needed support in the other; and that Sidney's earnest love should have more deeply impressed a heart naturally susceptible to anything that was honest and true.

And yet Harriet grew paler, and looked disturbed in mind, and Sidney Hinchford came home from business every day with a deeper shade of thought upon his face. He went less often to Camberwell also—she took notice of that—and stayed up late at night in the drawing-room, after having deluded his father into the belief that he should be only a few moments after him. All was mystery in Suffolk Street, denser than the fogs which crept thither so often in the winter time.

Mr. Wesden, before retiring from business, had left strict orders with Mattie to be the last to go round the house, and see, in particular, to the gas burners, and the bolts which Ann Packet was continually leaving unfastened, and had once received warning for in Mr. Wesden's time. Mattie had injunctions to see to the drawing-room burners as well; to wait to an hour however late for the Hinchford exit.

This waiting up became a serious matter when Sidney Hinchford remained in the drawing-room till the small hours of the morning, and brooded over his papers, with which one table or another was invariably strewn. Mattie, a young woman of business, who did a fair day's work, and rose early, ventured to remonstrate at last; it was intrenching beyond her province, but she made the plunge in a manner very nervous and new to her—in a manner that even confused herself a little.

He brought the remonstrance upon himself by coming down into the shop to hunt for some writing paper, which he intended to pay for in the morning, and was a little surprised to find Mattie sewing briskly in the back parlour.

"Up still, Mattie!—late hours for you," he said.

"Ah! and for you, too, sir."

"Men can do with little rest, and I never leave one day's work for the next," said he, in that quick manner which had become habitual to him, and which appeared, to strangers, tinged with more abruptness than was really intended. "I was thinking of robbing your stationery drawer, Mattie, and lo the thief is detected in the act."

"Oh! I hope you do not intend any more work to-night, sir."

"Why not?" he asked, his eyes expressing a mild sort of surprise through his spectacles.

"I'm waiting to see the gas out in that table-lamp."

"Can't I see to it myself?"

"I thought so until I found the tap in the india-rubber pipe turned full on last night."

"Did you sit up last night, too?"

"Mr. Wesden has always wished that I should make sure everything was safe."

"But I'm busy just now; you mustn't be a slave as well as myself."

"I hope you're not a slave, Mr. Sidney," said Mattie, assuming that half-familiar style of conversation which was natural to her with her two old friends, and which always escaped in spite of of her, "or that you will not keep one much longer, for it's not improving your looks, I can tell you."

"*You* can tell me," said Sidney; "well, what's the matter with my looks, Mattie?"

Mattie looked steadily at him.

"You're paler than you used to be," she said after a while; "you're not like yourself; you've something on your mind."

Sidney frowned, rubbed his hair up the wrong way, after his father's fashion, cleared off suddenly and then laughed.

"Who hasn't?" was his reply.

"There's nothing which can't easily be got over, or my name isn't Mattie," said our heroine, with great firmness.

She was full of her one reason for all this thought on his side, and the confusion and perplexity on Harriet's, and she delivered her hint emphatically.

"I don't despair of getting over most things," he said, with a forced lightness that did not deceive his observer; "there's only one thing in the way that bothers me."

He said it more to himself than Mattie, who cried, instinctively—

"What's that, sir?"

"Why, that's my secret," he responded, shutting up on the instant; "and I shall keep it till the last."

He had turned very stern and rigid; Mattie felt that she had crossed the line of demarcation, and withdrew into herself and her needlework with a sigh.

Sidney Hinchford shook himself away from that dark thought instanter.

"You're as curious as ever, Mattie—you'll be a true woman. I would not be your husband for the world."

Mattie felt herself crimson on the instant, and a strange wild commotion in her heart ensued, more unaccountable than the mystery which had deepened around her. They were light, idle words of his, but they made her cheeks flush and her bosom heave; he spoke in jest, almost in sarcasm, but the words rang in her ears as though he had thundered them forth with all the power of his lungs.

When all this Suffolk Street life was over; when she and he, when she and they whom she loved had gone their separate ways, when she was an old woman, she remembered Sidney Hinchford's words.

Still she flashed back the jesting reply—or whatever it was—with a quickness that was startling.

"You'll wait till you're asked," she said.

At this moment some one knocked at the outer-door.

"Hollo!—a late customer like me," said Sidney, opening the door as he was nearer to it, and then staring with surprise at the person who had arrived—no less a person than Mr. Wesden himself.

"Hollo!" he said again; "nothing wrong, sir, I hope?"

"Not at home," was the dry response. "Is anything wrong here?"

"Oh! no."

He entered, took the door-handle from Sidney, and closed the door himself, turned the key in the lock, and drew the bolts to. Sidney Hinchford thought Mr. Wesden looked very nervous that evening—very different from his usual stolid way.

"You're quite sure—quite sure that it's all right, sir?" asked Sidney, his thoughts flashing to Harriet again.

"I said so; I never tell an untruth, Sidney. Good night"

"Good night, sir. Oh!" turning back, "the letter-paper, Mattie—I had forgotten."

Mr. Wesden watched the transfer of the writing paper from the drawer to Sidney Hinchford's hands, glanced furtively from Sidney to Mattie, gradually unwinding a woolen comforter from his neck meanwhile.

When Sidney had withdrawn, very much perplexed, but too dignified to ask any more questions, Mr. Wesden turned to Mattie.

"What's he doing down here at this time of night, Mattie?"

"He came for writing paper—he's very busy."

"What are *you* sitting up for?"

"To see to the gas-burners in the drawing-room."

"Turn the gas off at the meter, and leave him in the dark next time," said Mr. Wesden. "You can go to bed now. I'll sit up for a little while; I'm going to sleep here to-night."

"Indeed, sir! Oh! sir, I hope that nothing serious *has* happened?"

"Nothing at all. It's not so very wonderful that I should come to my own house, I suppose, Mattie?"

"N—no," she answered, hesitating; "but it's past one o'clock."

"I couldn't sleep—and Harriet was at home with the good lady," he said, as if by way of excuse; adding very sulkily, a moment afterwards, "I never could sleep in that Camberwell place—I wish I'd never left the shop!"

Mr. Wesden hazarded no further reason for his eccentric arrival, and Mattie went up-stairs to lay it with the rest of her stock of mysteries daily accumulating round her. Mr. Wesden remained down-stairs, fidgeting with shop drawers, counting the money left in the till, and wandering up and down in a reckless, hypochondriacal fashion, very remarkable in a man of his phlegmatic temperament, and which it was as well for Mattie not to have seen.

Finally he groped his way down-stairs into the kitchen, and the coal-cellar where the gas-meter was placed, and with a wrench cut off the supply of gas for that night, casting Sidney Hinchford so suddenly into darkness, that he leaped up with an exclamation far from appropriate to his character.

"What the devil next?"

The next thing for Sidney was to knock over the chair he had been sitting upon, which came down on the drawing-room floor with a bumping noise that shook the house, and woke up his father, who shouted forth his name.

"Coming, coming," said Sidney, walking into the double-bedded room, and giving up further study or brooding for that night.

"What's the matter, Sid, my boy?" asked the father, from the corner; "haven't you been in bed yet?"

"Must have fallen asleep in the next room, I think."

"And a terrible row you've made in waking, Sid. Good night, my boy—God bless you!"

The old gentleman turned on his side, and was soon indulging in the snores of the just again. There was a night-light burning there, and Sidney took it from its saucer of water and held it above his head, looking down at that old, world-worn, yet handsome face of the father.

"God bless *you*!" he said, re-echoing his father's benediction; "how will you bear it when the time comes, I wonder?"

CHAPTER VI.

A BURST OF CONFIDENCE.

Yes, Mr. Wesden, late of Suffolk Street, had become nervous and eccentric in his old age—many people do, besides stationers. He had retired from business too late to enjoy the relaxation from business cares; he had better have died in harness than have given up the shop, for isolation therefrom began to work its evil.

He had not had much to worry him in his middle age; his youth had been a struggle, but he had been young and strong to bear with it, blest by a homely and affectionate wife, who struggled with him and consoled him; then had followed for more years than we care to reckon just now, the everyday life of a London shopkeeper—a life of business-making and money-making, plodding on in one groove, with little change to distract his attention, or trouble his brain. All quiet and monotonous, but possessing for John Wesden peace of mind, which, if not exactly happiness, was akin to it. And now in his old age, when every habit had been burned into him as it were, business was over, and idleness became a sore trial to him. And then after idleness came his daughter to worry him, not to mention Mattie, who worried him most of all, for reasons which we shall more closely particularize a chapter or two hence.

So with these troubles bearing all at once upon a mind that had been at its ease in its stronger days, Mr. Wesden turned eccentric. Want of method rendered him fidgety, the mysteries in *his* path, as well as Mattie's, perplexed him; he was verging upon hypochondriacism without being aware of it himself; and that suspicious nature which had been born with him, began to develop itself more, and give promise of bearing forth bitter fruit. Possibly before his concern for his daughter's health, was his concern for the shop in Great Suffolk Street, which he considered that he had neglected in leaving to the charge of a girl not eighteen years of age, and which, since the robbery, was an oppression that weighed heavily upon him. He was full of fancies concerning that shop; his mind—which unfortunately was fed by fancies at that time—began to give way somewhat when he took it in his head to think something had happened, at twelve o'clock at night, and start at once for Great Suffolk Street, as we have noticed in our preceding chapter.

The ice once broken, the eccentricities of Mr. Wesden did not diminish; he had his old bed-room seen to in the house again, and surprised Mattie more than once after this by sudden appearances at untimely hours. He had a right to look after his business—did *people* think that he had lost his interest in the shop, because he lived away from it?—did *people* think that he was not sharp enough for business still? With these changes he became more nervous, more irritable, and less considerate; yet brightening up sometimes for weeks together, and becoming his old stolid self again, to the relief of his wife and daughter. That daughter detected the change in her father also, woke up at last to the fact that her own thoughtfulness had tended to unsettle him, and became more like her old self also—or rather, more of an actress, with the power to impersonate that self from which she had seceded.

Everything was going wrong with our characters, when Harriet Wesden broke through the ice one night with that impulsiveness which she had not lived down or grown out of. It was strange that she always broke down in Mattie's presence; that only in the company of the stray did she feel the wish to avow all, and seek counsel in return. To Harriet Wesden the impulse was incomprehensible, but it was beyond her strength, at times, and carried her away. She loved Mattie; she saw in her the faithful friend rather than the servant; she knew that the child's passionate love for her had grown with Mattie's growth, and absorbed her being. But love was but half the reason with Harriet, and she would not own—which was the secret—that the weak and timid nature sought relief from a mind that had grown strong and practical in a rough school.

A need of sympathy, a perplexity becoming greater every day, allied to a love for the confidante, brought about the truth, which escaped in the old fashion.

She had been paying her visit—an afternoon one in this instance—to Mattie at the shop; it was a dull season, and no business stirring; the December gloom preyed upon the spirits of most people abroad that day; it affected Harriet more than usual, or the pressure of the old thoughts reduced her to subjection at last. The two girls were sitting by the fireside, Mattie with her face turned to the shop door, when Harriet Wesden laid both her hands suddenly on our heroine's.

"Mattie," she cried, "look me in the face a moment!"

"Come round to the little light there is left, then."

"There!"

Harriet Wesden set her pretty face, pale and anxious then, more into the light required. Mattie regarded it attentively.

"Isn't it a false face?" asked Harriet, in an excited manner—"the face of one who brings sorrow and wrong to all who know her?"

"I hope not."

"It is!" she asserted. "Oh! Mattie, I am in distress, and terrible doubt—I have been foolish, and acted inconsiderately—I am in a maze, that becomes more tangled with every step I take—tell me what to do!"

"You ought to know best, dear—you should not have any troubles which you are afraid to confess to your father and mother, and—and Mr. Hinchford."

"Yes, yes, but not to them first of all," she cried. "Oh! Mattie, I am not a wicked girl, God knows—I have never had a thought of wickedness—I would like everybody in the world to be as happy as I was once myself."

"Once!" repeated Mattie. "Oh! I won't have that."

"I don't think," she added, very thoughtfully regarding the fire, "that I shall be ever happy again. Now, Mattie dear, I'm going to swear you to secrecy, and then ask what you would do in my place."

"You're very kind to trust in me—but is there no one else?—Miss Eveleigh, for instance."

"She's a worse silly than I am!"

"Your mother."

"I should frighten her to death—she and father are both weak, and altering very much. Oh! Mattie, if they should die and leave me alone in the world!"

"Need you get nervous about that just now?"

"I'm nervous about everything—I'm unsettled—Mattie, I have acted very treacherously to *him*."

"To Mr. Sidney!—not to Mr. Sidney?"

"Yes," was the answer.

Mattie became excited. How had it occurred?—who had done it?—who had stolen her thoughts away from him?

"I have been trying very hard to love him—sometimes I think I do love him better than the—the *other*—just for a while, when he is very happy sitting near me, and very full of the future, that can never, never come."

"Go on please," said the curious Mattie.

"Mattie, you remember Mr. Darcy?" she asked, spasmodically.

"Mr. Darcy—no," said the puzzled Mattie.

"The gentleman who—who fell in love with me when I was a child," she explained, very rapidly, and with still greater excitement, "whom I thought I had forgotten, and who had forgotten me, until I met him again."

"Oh! this *is* wrong!" exclaimed Mattie.

"I know it—I have owned it!" cried Harriet; "let me tell the story out. I met him, parted coldly from him, met him again, all by accident on my part; met him for a third time at the Eveleighs, with whom he had got on visiting terms; met him day after day, evening after evening there, until the spell was on me which overpowered me, and robbed me of my peace—until I loved him, Mattie!"

"And he knows——"

"He knows nothing, save that I am engaged to be another's—and that I dare scarcely think of him."

"He knows too much, *I* know," said Mattie, reflectively; "and he has found a way to turn you against Mr. Sidney. What a wonder he must be!"

"Poor Sidney!"

"And to think it's all over between you and him," added Mattie—"him who thinks so much of you, and is growing old to my eyes, with the fear upon him which I understand now, and which is now so natural!"

"What fear!"

"Of losing you."

"I am so sorry—*so* very sorry for him. And I am ashamed to think that I have led him on to build his hopes upon me, and now must dash them down."

"Yes—to-night," said Mattie, thoughtfully.

"Tonight!" exclaimed Harriet, in alarm.

"I don't know much about these things—I never understood what love for a young man was, having had too much to do," she added, with a little laugh that echoed strangely in that shadowy room, "but it don't seem quite the thing to keep the two on, or both of them in suspense about you."

"Do you think I would?" asked Harriet, proudly.

"It seems to me that if I were in your place, I should take a pattern from Mr. Sidney, and speak out at once—go straight at it, as he calls it—and tell him everything."

"But——"

Mattie became excited in her turn.

"It isn't right—it isn't fair to let a man keep thinking of you, when you've turned against him," she cried; "it's cowardly and base to hide the truth from him, or be afraid of telling it. It won't kill him, Harriet, for he's a proud spirit, that will bear up through it all, bitterly as he will feel it for a while."

"I'm not afraid—it is not that," said Harriet; "I only wish to know what you would think the best method of telling him all, and yet sparing him pain. I have been fancying that if *you* hinted to him at first the truth——"

"*I* hint!" exclaimed Mattie, "not for the world. I'm only a servant here, and you might as well ask poor Ann Packet to hint the truth as me. I'm sorry—you will never know how sorry I am—that you two are going to break it off forever; but I should be more sorry still if you let to-night go by, and not try hard to face him."

"Mattie, I will face him," said Harriet, with her lips compressed; "I will tell him all. After all, it was not an engagement, and I was as free as he to make my choice elsewhere if I preferred. I am not in the wrong to tell him that my girlish fancy was a mistake."

"No—only in the wrong to keep the truth back."

"You will not think that I have intentionally attempted to deceive poor Sidney, will you?"

"God forbid, my dear."

"Vain—frivolous, and weak—anything but cruel. Yes, I will tell him all when he comes back to-night. There is no use in delay."

"Only danger," added Mattie, remembering her copy-book admonition; a copy which Sidney Hinchford had set her himself in the old days, when she was deep in text-hand.

"And then when it is all told, and he knows that I am free, happiness will come again, I suppose. Heigho! I was very happy once."

"Happiness will come again," said Mattie, more cheerfully, "to be sure."

"Mattie, I have been trying very hard to think of Mr. Sidney, first of all; it is that trying which has made me ill. I know he loves me very much, and will never think of anybody else; and it is—it is hard upon him now!"

"You must be very fond of this other one," said Mattie. "Is he handsome?"

"Very."

"And very fond of you, of course?"

"Yes; but it is a struggle to keep his love back—I am cold to him—and I—I will *not* listen to him, and so drive him to despair. Oh! I am a miserable wretch! I make everybody unhappy whom I meet."

The weak girl burst into tears, and rocked herself to and fro on the chair before the fire. Mattie passed her arms round her neck and drew the pretty agitated face to her bosom, soothing it there as though she had been a mother troubled with love-sick daughters of her own.

"It will soon be over now," Mattie said, when Harriet was more composed. "Try and be calm; think of what you shall say to poor Sidney, while I attend to the shop a bit."

Mattie went into the shop, leaving Harriet Wesden with her chin clutched in both hands, looking dreamily at the fire. She was more composed now the whole truth had escaped her; she felt that she should be happy in time, after Sidney Hinchford had been told all, and that terrible ordeal of telling it had been gone through. One more scene, which had made her shudder to forestall by sober thought, and then the new life, brighter and rosier from that day!

Poor Sidney, what should she say to him, to soften the look which would rise to his dark eyes and transfix her? What was best to say and do, to keep him from thinking ill of her, and despising her for vacillation?

Mattie came in, looking white and scared; but Harriet, possessed by a new thought which had suddenly dashed in upon her, failed to observe the change.

"Mattie, dear," she cried, "if he should think I give him up because he's poorer than Mr. Darcy—that it is for the sake of money that I turn away from him!"

"Money's a troublesome thing," said Mattie, snatching up her bonnet from the sideboard, and putting it on her head with trembling hands; "if you take your eyes from it for an instant, it's gone."

"But, Mr. Darcy——"

"Oh! bother Mr. Darcy," was the half-peevish exclamation. "I have been listening to you, and they've robbed the shop again. Everything's against me just now! Mind the place till I come back, please."

CHAPTER VII.

THE PLAN FRUSTRATED.

Yes, the house in Great Suffolk Street had been again visited by "the dangerous classes." It was a house well watched, or a house that was doomed to be unfortunate in its latter days. A house left in charge of a girl of seventeen, therefore likely to have its weak points, and considered worth watching in the dark hours. This was Mattie's idea upon awakening to the conviction of a second successful attempt upon Mr. Wesden's property; but Mattie was wrong.

The robbery was the result of accident and neglect, as most robberies are in this world. A youth had entered the shop to make a small purchase, and hammered honestly on the counter with the edge of his penny piece—a youth of no principle, certainly, brought up ragged, dirty, ignorant, and saucy—a Borough boy. Fate and the devil contrived that Mattie should be absorbed in the love-story of Harriet Wesden at the time, and the boy finding no attention paid to his summons, looked over the shop blind, saw the rapt position of the parlour occupants, dropped upon his hands and knees like a lad brought up to the "profession," and slid insidiously towards the till, which he found locked and keyless. Fortune being against his possession of any current coin of the realm, the young vagabond turned his attention to stock, and in less time than it takes to sum up his defalcations, had appropriated and made off with a very large parcel underneath the counter—a parcel that Wiggins, wholesale stationers of Cannon Street, had just forwarded by London Parcels' Delivery Company to order of John Wesden, Esq., and which parcel had been found almost too large to decamp with.

Mattie thought no more of Harriet Wesden's troubles; here was a second instance of her carelessness—of her incapacity for business. What would Mr. Wesden think now; he who had been so cold and strange to her after the last robbery? And what did she deserve?—she who had had a trust committed to her and abused it.

Mattie did not give way to any ebullition of tears; she was a girl with considerable self-command, and only betrayed her agitation by her whiter face. She did all that lay in her power to remedy the great error, leaving Harriet Wesden in charge of the shop whilst she ran down Great Suffolk Street and towards the Borough, hoping to overtake the robber. Straight to Kent Street went Mattie; thieves would be sure to make for Kent Street—all the years of her honest life faded away like a dream, and she ran at once to the house of a receiver of stolen goods, a house that she had known herself in the old guilty past.

Her hand was on the latch of the door, when a policeman touched her on the arm,

"Do you want anything here?"

"I've been robbed of a large parcel—I thought they must have brought it here."

"Why here?"

"This is Simes's—this used to be Simes's—surely."

"Yes, and it's Simes's still; but nobody's been here with a parcel. You haven't been and left nobody in Mr. Wesden's shop?" was his inelegant query.

Mattie did not remark that the policeman knew her then; she was too excited by her loss.

"Mr. Wesden's daughter's there."

"Then you had better come round to the police-station, and state your loss, Miss."

Mattie thought so too; she went to the police station, mentioned the facts of the robbery, the nature of the parcel stolen, &c., and then returned very grave and disconsolate to Great Suffolk Street, to find three customers waiting to be served, Harriet turning over drawer after drawer in search of the goods required, and one woman waiting for change, which Harriet, having mislaid her own purse, and found the till locked, was unable to give her.

Mattie turned to business again, attended to the customers, and then re-entered the parlour.

"It cannot be helped, and I must make the best of it," said Mattie; "I don't mind the loss it is to me, who'll pay for it out of my own earnings, as I do the vexation it will be to your father."

"Leave it to me, Mattie," said Harriet; "when I go home this evening, I will tell him exactly how it occurred, and how it was not your fault but mine. And, Mattie, I intend to pay for it myself, and not have your hard earnings entrenched upon."

"You're not in trust here," said Mattie, somewhat shortly; "if I don't pay for it, I shall be unhappy all my life."

"Then it's over and done with, and I wouldn't fret about it," said Harriet, suddenly finding herself in the novel position of comforter.

"I never fret—and I said that I would make the best of it," replied Mattie, placing her chair at the parlour door, half within the room and half in the shop; "and if I'm ever tricked again whilst I remain here, it's very odd to me."

Harriet Wesden, not much impressed by so matter-of-fact event as a robbery, was anxious to return to the subject which more closely affected herself; the parcel, after all, was of no great value; the police were doubtless looking for the thief; let the matter be passed over for the present, and the great distress of her unsettled mind be once more gravely dwelt upon! This was scarcely selfishness—for Harriet Wesden was not a selfish girl—it was rather an intense craving for support in the hard task of shattering another's hopes.

They had tea together in that little back parlour, and Harriet found it difficult work to keep Mattie's thoughts directed to the subject upon which advice had been given before the theft.

"You will not think of me," she said at last, reproachfully; "and what does it matter about that rubbishing parcel?"

"What can I do for you, more?" asked Mattie, wearily. Her head ached very much with all the excitement of that day, and she was inwardly praying for the time to pass, and the boy to put the shutters up. The robbery was *not* of great importance, and she wondered why it troubled her so much, and rendered her anxiety for others, just for a while, of secondary interest. Did she see looming before her the shadow of her coming trial; was there foreknowledge of all in store for her, stealing in upon her that dark December's night? She was superstitions enough to think so afterwards, when the end had come and life had wholly changed with her!

After tea, Mattie's impression became less vivid, for Harriet's nervousness was on the increase. The stern business of life gave way to the romance—stern enough also at that time—of Harriet Wesden. It was close on seven o'clock, and every minute might bring the well-known form and figure home.

"I shan't know what to say," said Harriet; "it seems out of place to ask him in here, and coolly begin at once to tell him not to think of me any more, just as he comes home from business, tired and weary, too, poor Sid! Shall I write to him?—I'll begin the letter now, and leave it here for you to give him. Oh! I can't face him—I shall never be able to face him, and tell him how fickle-minded I am!"

"Write to him if you wish then, Harriet; perhaps it is best, and will spare you both some pain."

"Yes, yes, I'll write," said Harriet, opening Mattie's desk instantly, and sending its neatly arranged contents flying right and left; "it *is* much the better way—why make a scene of it?—I hate scenes! And I'm not fickle-minded, Mattie," suddenly reverting to her self-accusation of a moment since; "for I had a right to think for myself, and choose for myself—we were not to be engaged till next month; and I did like him once—I do now, somehow! If *he* will only think well of me afterwards, and not despise me, poor fellow, and believe that I had a right to turn away from him, if my heart said that I was not suitable for him at the last. If he—Mattie, *where* do you keep your pens?"

Mattie remarked that she had turned the box full amongst the letter-paper. Harriet sat herself down to write the letter after much preparation and agitation; Mattie looked at her, sitting there, in the full light of the gas above her head, and thought how pretty a *child* she looked—how unfit to cope with the world's harshness—how lucky for her that she was the only child of parents who had made money for her, and so smoothed one road in life at least. Yes, more a child than a woman even then; captious, excitable, easily influenced, swayed by a passing gust of passion like a leaf, trembling at the present, at the future, always unresolved, and yet always, by her trust and confidence in others, even by her sympathy for others, to be loved.

Mattie went into the shop, leaving Harriet to compose her epistle; after a while, and when she was brooding on the parcel again, and wondering if Mrs. Watts were at the bottom of the robbery, Harriet called her. She took her place again on the neutral ground, between parlour and shop, and found Harriet very much discomfited; her face flushed, her fair hair ruffled about her ears, her blue eyes full of tears.

"I don't know what to say—I can't think of anything that's kind enough, and good enough for *him*. What would you say, Mattie?"

"And you that have had so much money spent on your education to ask me—still a poor, ignorant, half-taught girl, Miss Harriet!"

"I'm too flurried to collect my thoughts—I *can't* think of the right words," she said; "I can't tell him of Mr. Darcy before Mr. Darcy has spoken to me—and I—I don't like to write down that I—I don't love him—never did love him—it looks so spiteful, dear! Mattie, what would you say?"

"I should simply tell him the story which you told me."

"He might show the letter to father and mother, who are anxious—oh! much more anxious than you fancy—to marry me to Sidney."

"They know his value, Harriet."

"And then it will all come at once to trouble them, instead of breaking it by degrees. Well, it's my fate. I must not keep it from them."

"No. How much have you written?"

"'Dear Sidney'—and—and the day of the month, of course. Oh! dear—here he is!"

Away went paper and pens into the desk again, and the desk cleared from the table, and turned topsy-turvy on to a chair.

"Oh! the top of the ink-stand's out—look here!—oh! what a mess there'll be!" cried Mattie.

Harriet reversed the desk.

"Perhaps it's not all spilt—I'm very sorry to have made such a mess of it, and—and it's only Sidney's father, after all. Don't tell him I'm here."

The old gentleman came into the shop, and nodded towards Mattie standing in the doorway.

"Has my boy come home?" he asked.

"Not yet, sir."

The father's countenance assumed a doleful expression on the instant—life without his boy was scarcely worth having.

"He's very late, then, for I'm late," looking at his watch; "I hope he hasn't been run over."

Mattie laughed at the expression of the father's fear.

"That's not likely, sir."

"People do get run over at times, especially in the City, and more especially near-sighted people. There's nothing to laugh at."

And rather offended at the manner in which his gloomy suggestion had been received, Mr. Hinchford senior passed through the side door into the passage. Mattie found Harriet at the desk again, picking out several sheets of paper saturated with ink, and arranging them of a row on the fender.

"More ink, dear—more ink!" she cried, impetuously; "I've thought of what to say. Don't keep me long without the ink."

Mattie replenished her ink-stand, and Harriet dashed into the subject with vigour, slackened after the first few lines, then came to a dead stop, and stared intently at the paper. Mattie went into the shop for fear of disturbing Harriet's train of ideas, remained there an hour attending to customers, and arranging stock, finally went back into the parlour.

The desk was closed once more; a heap of torn papers was on the floor. Harriet, with her bonnet and shawl on, and her eyes red with weeping, was pacing up and down the room.

"No letter?" asked Mattie.

"I can't write a letter, and tell him what a wretch I am," she said, "and if I face him to-night, I shall drop at his feet. Girl," she cried, passionately, "do you think it is so easy to act as I have done, and then avow it?"

"I should not be ashamed to own it," was Mattie's calm answer; "I should consider it my duty to tell him."

"And I will tell him all. God knows I would not deceive him for the world, Mattie, or leave him in ignorance of the true state of my heart. But I cannot tell him now. I'm afraid!"

There was real fear in her looks—an intense excitement, that even alarmed Mattie. She saw, after all, that it was best to keep the secret back for that night.

"Then I would go home, Harriet, at once. To-morrow, when you are calmer, you may be able to write the letter."

"Yes, yes—to-morrow I will write it. I shall have all day before me, and can tear up as many sheets as I like. I will write it to-morrow, and post it from Camberwell. Mattie, as I'm a living woman, and as I pray to be free from this suspense and torture, I WILL write to him to-morrow!"

"One day is not very important," said Mattie, in reply, little dreaming of the difference that day would make. "Delays are dangerous—delays are dangerous"—she had written twenty times in her copy-book, and taken not to heart; and there *was* danger on its way to those who had put off the truth, and to him for whom they feared it.

"Delays are dangerous!" Take it to heart, O reader, and remember it in the hour when you shrink from the truth, as from a hot iron that may sear you. Wise old admonitions of our copy-book times—we might do worse very often than laugh at ye!

CHAPTER VIII.

A SUDDEN JOURNEY.

Harriet Wesden hurried away after her promise; Mattie, at the last moment, recalling to her notice the fact of the robbery, and reminding her of the way in which she ought to break the news to her father. Then the excited girl darted away to Camberwell, and it was like the stillness of the grave in the back parlour after her departure. Mattie went in for an instant to set the place to rights, and then returned to her watch in the shop, and to her many thoughts, born of that day's incidents. She was quite prepared for a visit from Mr. Wesden at a late hour, but Mr. Wesden's movements under excitement were not to be calculated upon; and we may say here that the knowledge of his loss did not bring him post-haste to Great Suffolk Street. Mattie was thinking of her loss, when the passage door opened, and the white head of Mr. Hinchford peered round and looked up at the clock, over the top shelf where the back stock was kept. The movement reminded Mattie of the time, and she glanced at the clock herself—*half-past nine.*

"I thought the clock had stopped up-stairs," he said, by way of explanation for his appearance.

"I had no idea it was so late," said Mattie.

"I had no idea it was so early," responded Mr. Hinchford; adding, after a pause, "though I can't think where the boy has got to; he said he would be home early, as he had some accounts to look through."

"It's not very late, sir, and if he has gone to Camberwell, not knowing Miss Harriet was here to-night——"

"He always comes home first—I never knew him go anywhere without coming home first to tell me. But," with another look at the clock, "it's not so very late, as you say, Mattie."

"He will be here in a minute."

"I hope so," said Mr. Hinchford, going to the shop door, and looking down the street, "for it's coming on to rain, and he has no umbrella. The boy will catch his death of cold."

After standing at the door for two or three minutes, the old gentleman turned to go up-stairs again.

"It'll be a thorough wet night—I'll tell Ann to keep plenty of water in the boiler—nothing like your feet in hot water to stave off a cold."

He retired. Half an hour afterwards he reappeared in the shop, excitable and fidgety.

"I can't make it out," he said, after another inspection of the clock; "there's something wrong."

"Perhaps he has gone to the play, sir."

"Pooh! he hates plays," was the contemptuous comment to this; "he wouldn't waste his time in a playhouse. No, Mattie there's something wrong."

"I don't think so," said Mattie, cheerfully. "I would not worry about his absence just yet, sir."

"I'll give him another hour, and then I'll go down to the office and ask after him."

"Or find him there, sir."

"No, they're not busy, I think. He can't be there. Mattie," he said suddenly. "Have you noticed a difference in him lately?"

"I—I fancy he seems, perhaps, a little graver; but then he's growing older and more manly every day."

"Ah! he grows a fine fellow—there isn't such another boy in the world—perhaps it's all a fancy of mine, after all."

Mattie knew that it was no fancy; that even Sidney's care and histrionic efforts could not disguise his trouble entirely from the father. But she played the part of consoler to Mr. Hinchford as well as she was able, and the old gentleman, less disturbed in mind, returned to his room for the second time.

But time stole on, and Mattie herself found a new anxiety added to those which had heretofore disturbed her. The wet night set in as Mr. Hinchford had prophesied; the boy came and put up the shutters; the clock ticked on towards eleven; all but the public-houses were closed in Great Suffolk Street, and there were few loiterers about.

Ann Packet brought in the supper, and was informed of the day's two features of interest—the robbery, and the absence of Mr. Sidney. Ann Packet, of slow ideas herself, and slower still in having other ideas instilled into her, thought that the missing parcel was connected with the missing lodger, and so conglomerated matters irremediably.

"You may depend upon it, Mattie, he'll bring the parcel back—it's one of his games—he was a rare boy for tricks when I knew him fust."

"Ann, you've been asleep," said Mattie, sharply.

"I couldn't help it," answered Ann, submissively; "it was very lonely down there, with no company but the *beadles*—and times ain't as they used to was, when you could read to me, and was more often down there."

"Ah! times are altering," sighed Mattie.

"And Mr. Wesden don't like me here till after the shop's shut—because he can't trust me, or I talk too much, I s'pose," she said; "but now, dear, sit down and tell me all about everything, to keep my sperits up."

Ann Packet and Mattie always supped together after the shop was closed—Ann Packet lived for supper time now, looked forward all the day to a "nice bit of talk" with the girl who had won upon those affections which three-fourths of her life had rusted from disuse.

"It's uncommon funny that I never had anybody to care about afore I knowed you, Mattie," she said regularly, once or twice a-week; "no father, mother, sisters, anybody, till you turned up like the ace in spekkilation. And now, let me hear you talk, my dear—I don't fancy that your tongue runs on quite so fast as it did."

Ann Packet curled herself in her chair, hazarded one little complaint about her ankles, which were setting in badly again with the Christmas season, and then prepared to make herself comfortable, when once more Mr. Hinchford appeared, with his hat, stick, and great cloak this time.

"Mattie, I can't stand it any longer—I'm off to the office in the City."

Mattie did not like the look of his excited face.

"I'd wait a little while longer, sir."

"No—something has happened to the boy."

"Shall I go with you, sir?"

"God bless the girl!—what for?"

"For company's sake—it's late for you to be alone, sir."

"Don't you think I can take care of myself?—am I so old, feeble, and drivelling as that? Are they right at the office, after all?" he added in a lower tone.

"I shouldn't like to be left here all alone," murmured Ann Packet; "particularly after there's been robberies, and——"

There was the rattle of cab-wheels in the street, coming nearer and nearer towards the house.

"Hark!" said Mattie and Mr. Hinchford in one breath.

The rattling ceased before the door, the cab stopped, Mr. Hinchford pointed to the door, and gasped, and gesticulated.

"Open, o—open the door!—he has met with an accident!"

"No, no, he has only taken a cab to get here earlier, and escape the wet," said Mattie, opening the door with a beating heart, nevertheless.

Sidney Hinchford, safe and sound, was already out of the cab and close to the door. Mattie met him with a bright smile of welcome, to which his sombre face did not respond. He came into the shop, stern and silent, and then looked towards his father.

"I thought you might have gone to bed, father," he said.

"Bed!" ejaculated Mr. Hinchford, in disgust; "what has—what has——"

"Come up-stairs, I wish to speak to you."

Father and son went up-stairs to their room, leaving Mattie at the open door. The cab still remained drawn up there; the cabman stood by the horse's head, stolid as a judge in his manifold capes.

"Are you waiting for anything?" asked Mattie.

"For the gemman, to be sure."

"Going back again?"

"He says so—I spose it's all right," he added dubiously; "you've no back door which he can slip out of?"

"Slip out of!" cried the disgusted Mattie, slamming the front door in his face for his impudent assertion.

Meanwhile Sidney Hinchford was facing his father in the drawing-room.

"Sit down and take the news coolly, sir," he said; "there's nothing gained by putting yourself in a flurry."

"N—no, no, my boy, n—no."

"I have no time to spare, and I wish to leave you all right before I go."

"Go!"

"I am going for a day or two, very likely for a week, on a special mission for my employers—that is all that I can tell you without breaking the confidence placed in me—I must go at once."

"Bless my soul! what—what can I possibly do without you. Can't I go with you? Can't I—"

"You can do nothing but wait patiently for my return, believing that I am safe, and taking care of myself. Why, what are a few days?"

"Well, not much after all," said the father, wiping his forehead with his silk-handkerchief, "and there's no danger, of course?"

"Not any."

"And you are only going——"

"A journey of a few days. Try and calm yourself whilst I pack a few things in my portmanteau. There, that's well!"

Sidney passed into the other room, leaving his father still struggling with the effects of his astonishment. The portmanteau must have been filled without any regard for neatness, for Sidney in a few minutes returned with it in his hands.

"Why, you should be proud of this journey of mine," he said with a forced lightness that could only have deceived his father; "think what it is to be chosen out of the whole office to undertake this business."

"It's a good sign. Yes, I see that now."

"And I shall be back sooner than you expect, perhaps. Why, you and I must not part like two silly girls, to whom the journey of a few miles is the event of a life. Now, good-bye, sir—God keep you strong and well till I come back again!"

"And you, my lad, and you, too."

"Amen. God grant it."

There was a strange earnestness in the son's voice, but the father was still too much excited to take heed.

"And now good-bye again," shaking his father's hands; "you'll stay here, sir, you'll not come down any more to-night."

"Yes, I will."

"You must try and keep calm; I will beg you as a favour to remain here, father."

"Well, well, if you wish it—but I'm not a child."

Sidney released his father's hands, caught up his portmanteau, and marched down stairs. Mattie, pale with suppressed excitement, met him in the shop. He put down his burden, caught her by the wrist, and drew her into the parlour. Seeing Ann Packet there, he bade her go down stairs somewhat abruptly, released his grip of Mattie, and waited for Ann's withdrawal, beating his foot impatiently upon the carpet.

Mattie looked nervously towards him, and thought that she had never seen him look more stern and hard. His face was deathly white, and his eyes burned like coals behind the glasses that he wore.

"Mattie," he said, "you and I, my father and you, are old friends."

"Yes, sir."

"I will ask a favour of you before I go. Take care of him! Ask him to come down here to smoke his pipe with you, and keep him as light-hearted as you can till I return."

"Who?—I, sir?"

"You have the way with you; you are quick to observe, and it will not take much pains to keep him pleased, I think. When he begins to wonder why I haven't returned, break to him by degrees that I have deceived him, fearing the shock too sudden for his strength."

"Oh! sir, how can you leave all this to me?"

"I have faith in no one else, Mattie, to do me this service. You are always cool, and will know the best way to proceed. Cheer up the old gentleman all you can, too;—you were a quaint girl once—don't let him miss me if you can help it."

"And you'll be gone——"

"Six weeks or two months."

"It's not a very happy journey, sir."

"How do you know that?" was the quick rejoinder.

"You're not looking happy—there's trouble in your face, Mr. Sidney."

"Well, there is room for it, and I am going, as I fear, to face trouble, and bring back with me disappointment. We can't have it all our own way in this world, Mattie."

"No, sir, that's not likely."

"And if there be more troubles than one ahead, why we must fight against them till we beat them back, or they—crush us under foot. Good-bye."

He shook hands with her long and heartily, adding, "You will remember your trust—you will break the news to him like a daughter?"

"I'll do my best, sir."

"He knows that I cannot send him any letters."

"And, and—letters for you?"

She thought of the letter which Harriet Wesden, in her sleepless bed, might be pondering upon then. Of the new trouble which he seemed to guess not; for immediately afterwards he said—

"Keep the letters till I come back—and give my love to Harriet; tell her I shall think of her every hour of the day and night. I wrote to her the last thing this evening. Now, good-bye, old girl, and wish me luck."

"The best of luck, Mr. Sidney—with all my heart!"

"Luck in the distance—luck when I come back again, and see it shining in my Harriet's eyes. Ah! *it won't do!*" he added, with a stamp of his foot.

"I'll pray for it sir," cried Mattie; "we can't tell what may happen for the best, or what *is* for the best, however it may trouble us at first."

"Spoken like the parson at the corner shop," he said, a little irreverently. "Bravo, Mattie—honest believer!"

He passed from the shop into his cab, glancing at the up-stairs windows, and waving his hand for a moment towards his father, waiting anxiously there to see the last of him.

The cab rattled away the moment afterwards, and Sidney Hinchford was borne on his unknown journey.

On the evening of the next day, a letter, in Harriet Wesden's hand-writing, was received. The postman and Mr. Hinchford, senior, came into the shop together.

"Sidney Hinchford, Esq.," said the postman.

"Thank you—I'll post it to him when he sends me his address," said Mr. Hinchford. "By Jove!" looking at the superscription, "the ladies miss him already."

Harriet Wesden had kept her promise, and found courage to write her story out.

END OF THE FIRST VOLUME.

CPSIA information can be obtained
at www.ICGtesting.com
Printed in the USA
LVHW031738010323
740520LV00003B/806

9 789356 901629